# Letters to His Beloved

For the Single Girls Navigating
Their Way through
This Ordained Season

## Alyssa Phillips

WESTBOW
PRESS®
A DIVISION OF THOMAS NELSON
& ZONDERVAN

WestBow Press books may be ordered through booksellers or by contacting:

WestBow Press
A Division of Thomas Nelson & Zondervan
1663 Liberty Drive
Bloomington, IN 47403
www.westbowpress.com
1 (866) 928-1240

Because of the dynamic nature of the Internet, any web addresses or links contained in this book may have changed since publication and may no longer be valid. The views expressed in this work are solely those of the author and do not necessarily reflect the views of the publisher, and the publisher hereby disclaims any responsibility for them.

Any people depicted in stock imagery provided by Getty Images are models, and such images are being used for illustrative purposes only. Certain stock imagery © Getty Images.

Unless otherwise indicated, all Scripture quotations taken from the New American Standard Bible® (NASB), Copyright © 1960, 1962, 1963, 1968, 1971, 1972, 1973, 1975, 1977, 1995 by The Lockman Foundation Used by permission. www.Lockman.org

Scripture quotations marked (NIV) are taken from the Holy Bible, New International Version®, NIV®. Copyright © 1973, 1978, 1984, 2011 by Biblica, Inc.™ Used by permission of Zondervan. All rights reserved worldwide. www.zondervan.comThe "NIV" and "New International Version" are trademarks registered in the United States Patent and Trademark Office by Biblica, Inc.™

ISBN: 978-1-9736-8312-4 (sc)
ISBN: 978-1-9736-8311-7 (hc)
ISBN: 978-1-9736-8313-1 (e)

Library of Congress Control Number: 2020900361

Print information available on the last page.

WestBow Press rev. date: 01/13/2020

This collection of letters is dedicated to Jesus.
These words are His.
My story is His.
Your story is His.
The beauty of this life is His.

Dear Single Girl,

I don't know where this letter finds you. I don't know you personally. I don't know the precious details that make up your beautiful self. But I know the desire of your heart.

The fact that you are reading this means you don't have a man by your side. You may have just lost him. Your heart might be shattered into tiny pieces that consist of all your hopes and dreams with him, the past plans for your future life together, and the memories of him and his sweet smile. My teary-eyed single girl, my heart hurts for your heart, and I wish I could make the aching less sharp. But I alone cannot.

You may be between guys right now. You may actually always be between a relationship and a fling. You want so badly to be loved and to be some man's girl, but it never quite works out. To you, my short-lived single girl, please slow down. Wait to be pursued, and don't ever doubt your worth. You are beautiful.

You may have always been single and have yet to find that right guy. You yearn so badly to have what all the girls around you have, but it never seems to come. Your independence has been forced upon you, and you rock that life, but deep down you don't want to *have* to be independent. You want to be taken care of. To you, my sassy and confident single girl, I see behind the strength. I see the vulnerability. I see the hopeless gaze. Hang on and don't give up hope. Your story isn't finished.

Whoever you are, I hear you. I see you in the grocery store with your cute and casual outfit and your shiny lip gloss, perusing the "meals for one" section. I see you at the gym in your brand-new stretchy pants and sarcastic tank top, pushing yourself to be a better and stronger you. I see you on social media with your new and updated profile picture, with your good hair day and picture-perfect makeup.

I see you ... because I am you. I completely understand the "I don't need no man" mantra that wars with the "I just want to be in love and have a family" wish.

You are not alone in this season. You are not the first girl to be the last of her friends to get married. You are not the first girl to eat a pint of ice cream because that boy you had a crush on forgot your name. You are not the first girl to get asked at every family event, "Why don't you have a boyfriend yet?"

Only some will understand these experiences and challenges. Some may laugh at the reality of what we single women go through, but I am going to lay it out there. I want to open up my heart to you, my sweet single friend, and share my story and my life. I love the fact that you're joining me on this journey. I know it is going to be beautiful.

—AP

*Alyssa Phillips*

# Purpose

Dear Single Girl,

Just for a moment, I want you to take a deep breath. Pause the anxiety, pause the worry, and pause the tears. That breath in your lungs, that calm sigh—that's life, sister friend. Today, in this hour, you are alive. Your precious heart is beating, and your face is still capable of a smile. Wherever this chapter finds you, it's found you alive. It's found you for a purpose.

I'm a firm believer in purpose. Everything created on this earth carries a unique purpose. The Lord Jesus was intentional with His creation. Every living thing was designed to live a life specifically laid out for its kind. Everything without a heartbeat has an equally monumental role as well. The sun that wakes us up each morning greets us with an everlasting promise of faithfulness. The mighty trees in my front yard stand proud and tall, offering shade for us down below and a home for the creatures above. The purple Sharpie pen I am using right now to write you this letter is serving its purpose by putting what you need to hear onto this paper.

The list will continue on for ages, but in everything there is purpose. Behind this purpose is the Master Orchestrator and Chief Engineer of it all. I do not know where you land on the issue of the Almighty God, but I do know you need Him. If you know Him, you need Him. If you don't know Him, you need Him. I know Him, but oh, how I need Him every hour. He is the source of my purpose. He is the fingerprint on everything I touch. He is the voice calling you from these pages. Without Him, I would have nothing of worth to offer you. So hear this now, sweet single girl. The God of this universe handcrafted that gentle heart of yours. He spent extra time molding it into a heart in need of great love. He designed your spirit to long for the purest of love stories. A love story that never ceases and carries you the rest of your life. That raw love story you crave can be yours to own. By the grace of Jesus Christ, your fragile heart can be whole. Just as He is the purpose, He is unfailing love Himself. He craves your heart and fights for your life. I pray this Jesus I write of is drawing you to Himself and to His cross. I pray that a divine revelation of your need for the Savior begins to blossom.

I say all of this because *this* is the truth. My life is forever marked by Jesus. My heart is forever taken by the King. I think about that summer evening so long ago in a gym, sitting in those bleachers when the painter of the stars in the sky found me in my deepest need and most desperate state. It was a time where I thought I could be good enough on my own, make it in this life without help, and aimlessly end up where I needed to be. I thought that I was okay and that I didn't or couldn't do wrong.

But on that night, someone authentic spoke to my heart. He told me that I needed to follow Jesus and rely on Him. He told me my sin was deep, my motives were selfish, and my heart was alone and would eternally remain alone unless He came in and took up residence. By calling upon the saving grace of Jesus and His sacrifice of death on that old, rugged cross for my own sin and despair, I could accept the truth He spoke so long ago.

> To open their eyes so that they may turn from darkness to light and from the dominion of Satan to God, that they may receive forgiveness of sins and an inheritance among those who have been sanctified by faith in Me. (Acts 26:18 NASB)

It all became clear. The longing I had always felt was intentional. That void had a purpose. That ache for something (and someone) bigger than me was set into motion ages ago. Jesus created me to be a broken girl in need of rescuing just so He could break through the chaos, pick up my weary soul, and whisper in His strong but quiet voice, "My love, I have you now. I am here. The past is behind us. Let's face the future together with My strength and My fortitude."

By surrendering to the Holy God that night and begging for my filthy sin to be taken from me, my life changed forever. I knew I belonged to someone. My heart was forever secure, and I was finally able to rest in the truth.

> But in all these things we overwhelmingly conquer through Him who loved us. For I am convinced that neither death, nor life, nor angels, nor principalities, nor things present, nor things to come, nor powers, nor height, nor depth, nor any other created thing, will be able to separate us from the love of God, which is in Christ Jesus our Lord. (Romans 8:37–39 NASB)

What a gift that night was. What a treasure it was to be given the ability to believe in the God who knit me together in the womb.

> For you formed my inward parts; you wove me in my mother's womb. I will give thanks to You, for I am fearfully and wonderfully made; wonderful are Your works, and my soul knows it very well. (Psalm 139:13–14 NASB)

So, my dear single girl, I firmly believe in this thing called purpose. We can go a step further and add a second word to it: *divine*. Divine purpose. The principle behind *divine* simply translates into something given or manifested from the Lord. It seems that everything around us has a hint—if not a blatantly obvious touch—of someone bigger than you or me. It's as if all circumstances, moments, and seasons are intertwined within some master plan. Our human vision is only capable of the here and now. But I assure you the bigger story is in motion, and you are invited to be a part of it.

This small collection of letters isn't the big picture, but I hope it will point you to the big picture. I hope, as you journey along with me, the ache you have deep down to your toes will cease and be replaced with a belonging and undeniable trust in the Almighty God and His sweet story for your life.

Being a single girl most assuredly has purpose. Each and every life has its unique plan, and through each story lies purpose. This season, this moment, this hour spent listening to my heart—none of this will be in vain. Relax, sister friend. You are going to be just fine.

# *It's Okay to Cry*

Dear Single Girl,

I hope you're having a good day today. I hope you woke up with a sweet smile on your face and a calm breeze singing over your heart. I hope the sun is shining and the birds are making melodies outside your window. I especially hope for all my fellow coffee lovers out there that your cup of warm and smooth goodness made that sweet smile of yours stretch just an inch wider and dig deeper into your soul.

With all of that said, I still see you, my dark-eyed and downcast single girl. I see that eye roll and those slumped shoulders. I see those tears hiding behind your beautiful eyes. I see you scoff as you read my hopes for your ability to have a good day. I get it. Your heart is void of the love you crave. Your picture frames are filled with you and your family and BFFs, not that guy who makes those butterflies have a dance party within you. You woke up with the other side of your bed cold and empty, the toilet seat down, and your television is still on *Say Yes to the Dress* instead of ESPN or *Cops*.

Most days, you continue on, and those realities don't bother you. You embrace the solitude with ease and find the good in flying solo. But some days it just gets to you. You look around at the absence of masculinity and wish so deeply there was a man by your side. Someone to laugh at the blunders you make in the kitchen. Someone to take the trash out because that's a boy's job. Someone to hang your shower curtain rod because, let's face it, those things are from the devil.

When your independence is wearing thin and you are at your limit, tears start to fill your eyes. You tell yourself to stop. You're frustrated that you're overwhelmed once again. The anger makes the tears fall harder and faster. And there you are, crying again. The trigger is new, but the heart issue is the same. You are a single girl in a culture where it feels as if the majority of women are spoken for by their beaus. You're mad. You're mad at your shower curtain rod for falling for the twelfth time in twenty minutes. You're mad that you have to talk to the air conditioner guy about your unit and have no clue what half the words he says mean. You're mad at those spiders for wanting to be your roommates, and you have to kick them out alone.

Sister, I understand these emotions. I am right there with you, crying and wiping my eyes alongside you. Don't let the enemy tell you those tears make you weak and silly. I assure you they make you human. They make you what you are: a precious soul who can't do it on her own. A sweet girl who wasn't meant to walk this side of heaven alone.

Let me tell you something, my capable but not that capable single girl – Jesus can be your hero and your most trusted friend. He absolutely knew you were going to have bad days, get overwhelmed, and have a mini breakdown every once in a while. Hear His strong whisper as He reminds you, "The Lord is near to the brokenhearted and saves those who are crushed in spirit" (Psalm 34:18 NASB).

*Alyssa Phillips*

As you're crying those tears, Jesus is sitting right beside you with His mighty arm around your shoulders, letting His presence heal your weary soul. He isn't fazed by your less than glamorous reality. In fact, He is so aware of your circumstances that he is orchestrating a beautiful song to be sung to the end of your tears. He is making beauty and hope spring forth from your desolation. The dust you are trekking through currently isn't forever, sweet girl. Remember that. Know that, yes, it is absolutely okay to cry, but this sadness cannot last forever. A man was never designed to fill your soul with acceptance and security. As your tears slow, remember that a new life in you from Jesus will make you abundantly whole and secure. You can have a forever need-meeter and problem-solver. Jesus has beautiful things for you *now*.

In this lonely season, He has Himself for you. He is all you need. Enough of Him is enough to let the word *lonely* fall from your vocabulary. He goes before and behind you, giving you a reason to dry the tears and let a smile live on your face. Chin up, buttercup. You aren't forgotten. You are cherished by the mightiest of Kings. Never forget He is in your corner, even on your darkest of days.

> Behold, God is my salvation. I will trust and not be afraid; for the Lord God is my strength and my song, and He has become my salvation. (Isaiah 12:2 NASB)

# You Matter

Dear Single Girl,

Can I speak something to you right quick? Can I cover you with a truth that your spirit needs to hear right now? If you take the time to seek the Lord each and every day, He is already pouring His love all over you, within you, and next to you ... all for you.

The last part of Zephaniah 3:17 (NASB), "He will rejoice over you with shouts of joy," should make you stop. Should make you breathe. Should make you listen to His still, small, but abounding voice. And because that same rejoicing Lord is using me as a simple mouthpiece, please let the eyes and ears of your heart hear what I have to say in these short moments.

You matter. Precious one, listen. You matter. You. The girl who might feel isolated in her friend group. You matter. The girl who has a closet full of bridesmaid dresses but lacks that white gown your heart desires. You matter. The girl who is working that eight-to-five job who isn't sure you're making a positive impact in this world. You matter.

I don't say this lightly to casually give you a tiny pep talk. The King of all kings, the God whose name is abundantly greater than any other name, is whispering but nonetheless proclaiming to you, my sweet sister, that you matter. The seventeenth verse in Psalm 139 (NASB) declares this anthem: "How precious also are your thoughts to me, O God! How vast is the sum of them!"

You are precious to the God who sends rain down to the earth and causes the ocean waves to roar. Oh, sweet girl, let this soak into the fibers of your soul. Let in that calming voice and hear Him say, "You matter."

You don't have to earn it. You don't have to be good enough. You don't have to know everything.

You matter.

You don't have to have a degree from an Ivy League university. You don't have to work within the most prestigiously ranked company. You don't have to have four or five or six figures in your checking account.

You matter.

Your heart is being aggressively pursued by a warrior King who will always rescue you and take care of you because you matter to Him. In whatever this season looks like to you—a job that isn't glorious; an apartment that has chipped paint and smells like feet; a car that barely makes it from point A to point B—I can assure you of one thing. If you are where the Lord has planted you and are letting Him sanctify you, pursue you, and teach you, even in that job that makes you tuck in your oversized polo into your belted khakis ... You matter. You matter within your less than desirable circumstances. He calls you in every moment to look to Him and praise His name.

Paul says it best in 1 Corinthians 10:31 (NASB): "Whether, then, you eat or drink or whatever you do, do all to the glory of God."

His glory matters to Him just as much as you matter to Him. And He didn't say *some* things for His glory. He said *all*. Each day you wake up, you matter to Him and have the honor to glorify Him in that seemingly mundane schedule of yours. If you start asking Jesus at the beginning of your day—before the chaos begins and that polo shirt gets tucked in—to show you the circle of influence around you and the needs that exist that He wants you to be a part of, you will see that you matter. Don't get crazy on me and think you are the solution and the bee's knees. You're not God, but you are loved so passionately by Him that He allows you the privilege to be a warrior for the kingdom of God. By His strength and His power, you matter to Him, and He matters above all.

> The God who made the world and all things in it, since He is Lord of heaven and earth, does not dwell in temples made with hands; nor is He served by human hands, as though He needed anything, since He Himself gives to all people life and breath and all things; and He made from one man every nation of mankind to live on all the face of the earth, having determined their appointed times and the boundaries of their habitation, that they would seek God, if perhaps they might grope for Him and find Him, though He is not far from each one of us; for in Him we live and move and exist, as even some of your own poets have said, "For we also are His children." (Acts 17:24–28 NASB)

You matter to Him, the One who chooses to give you a role in His story. Don't let the enemy tell you different. The enemy's voice will sell you short and discourage the fire out of you. But our gracious and sweet heavenly Father will use His Holy Spirit and guide you into all truth. He is the repairer of the broken. It's His specialty. Sister, please trust in that simple truth today.

You matter.

You can be used as a light today in a way only able to be done by you. Jesus gave you this season, this unique time, just for you. Look around and smile. God has a plan for you today.

# I'm Your Personal Cheerleader

Dear Single Girl,

I'm rooting for you. I want you to know that. I'm cheering you on in this crazy life and in this crazy culture that tells you there is something wrong with you if you don't have a man at your side. This same culture that makes you feel shame for not having a mate will, in the same breath, scream that you can and will accomplish everything without the help of a man. I'm sure your brain is tired of keeping up with how exactly you aren't meeting the expectations of this shifty culture on this specific day.

Sister friend, let me let you in on something that will hopefully rid you of playing the acceptance game with this world and free you from the horror of being picked last.

You weren't made for this world. You weren't designed to keep up with the fleeting whims of those who find their worth in being better than their neighbor. The relentless inconsistency of what goes in this life is merely based on opinion and originates from the one who opposes the Lord.

> He was a murderer from the beginning, and does not stand
> in the truth because there is no truth in him. Whenever
> he speaks a lie, he speaks from his own nature, for he is a
> liar and the father of lies. (John 8:44b NASB)

The enemy stirs up trouble in all avenues, but he especially enjoys the lies this world speaks to the children of the light. The lies that tempt you to waver from the One who gives you hope. The lies that push you to settle for mediocrity or reach for unattainable success that in no way nourishes your precious soul. The lies that contradict each other so often and so blatantly that it's hard to tell up from down.

> Be of sober spirit, be on the alert. Your adversary, the
> devil, prowls around like a roaring lion, seeking someone
> to devour. (1 Peter 5:8 NASB)

Beloved, hear this conquering truth.

> Jesus Christ is the same yesterday and today and forever.
> Do not be carried away by varied and strange teachings.
> (Hebrews 13:8–9a NASB)

Turn off that video blog. Quit scrolling through all the motivational pins on Pinterest. Don't listen to those ladies on talk shows or gossip shows. Stop reading those moronic self-help books and start opening up God's Word. He has no desire for us to equate His word with advice and simultaneously take into the account the advice of the hottest celebrity who believes only in herself and in science. Sorry not sorry for being so black and white here, sister. That mandate of God leaves no room for a gray area.

> For am I now seeking the favor of men, or of God? Or
> am I striving to please men? If I were still trying to please

men, I would not be a bond-servant of Christ. (Galatians 1:10 NASB)

I can see your pursed lips and your glaring eyes. My evil-eye-giving single girl, you can't have it both ways. You cannot in the least bit find your identity in what the world deems right if you are following Jesus. I understand why your emotions are all over the place: they are merely reacting to the unstable shifts in society's guide to finding security. You simply cannot serve Jesus and also serve the ideals of a self-promoting, self-driven, self-fulfilled culture. *We serve Him to be like Him.*

The lies of this world will tell you to be happy, be strong, never give up, have fun, fall in love, stay independent, love men, and love women. It is okay to keep making the same mistake because that is who you are. The lies and mantras of this world all have one thing in common: they don't have the voice of God within them. Scripture is not at the root of them. If Jesus is not within what you are being told, then it has no eternal value.

All things have been created through Him and for Him. He is before all things, and in Him all things hold together. (Colossians 1:16b–17 NASB; for full effect, the entire first chapter backs what I am rambling about here)

So, my precious friend, I say all of this to you because I honestly need to hear it too. This world needs more ladies to close off their ears to the multifaceted, destructive lies and behaviors and open up their hearts fully to Jesus. I need more ladies who stop finding their identity in the men next to them and stake all their worth in the Savior, who brought them out of darkness and into light. I need more ladies who will stop fretting that for yet another year, they don't have a valentine, and they begin to turn their eyes off of themselves and onto the heart of God.

Fewer girl bosses and more ladies. Less boasting and more

encouraging. Less pride and more dependence on Jesus. Less double-mindedness and more steadfastness to the truth.

As a final thought for this letter, I want to remind you that I'm cheering for you, and I'm praying specifically for your heart. Even more so, Jesus is cheering you on better than I am. The winds of this crazed society will continue to blow so heavily against you, my sweet, single girl. But if you kneel before the Word of God and invite His oh so Holy presence to keep inhabiting your soul, you won't be able to lose. Jesus wins every time. You will realize more and more that this earth is not our home and that all we need is His grace and love.

> But you are a chosen race, a royal priesthood, a holy nation, a people for God's own possession, so that you may proclaim the excellencies of Him who has called you out of darkness into His marvelous light; for you once were not a people, but now you are the people of God; you had not received mercy, but now you have received mercy. Beloved, I urge you as aliens and strangers to abstain from fleshly lusts which wage war against the soul. (1 Peter 2:9–11 NASB)

# Choose the Worthy Road

Dear Single Girl,

I see you sitting there, precious one. I see you reading this letter while covering up a yawn. I see that you're tired. Tired of picking up the slack in your life. Tired of trying to make a big life decision without the sounding board of a male leader who ultimately carries the heavier weight. Tired of being the checkbook boss and doing your best to keep your bills in order and on time. Tired of preparing meals for one which still somehow manages to make enough for a family of six including leftovers.

I hear you. And before you roll your eyes and assume this letter is going to tell you to "hang in there" and "it's really not that bad if you put your life into perspective," please listen to me, your fellow, tired, single girl. This season that you and I are in has its disadvantages. The single life isn't always glamorous. It isn't a party all the time, and neither is it the life filled with carefree days. Now, before you assume that I am going to RSVP to the single girl pity party, you're wrong. Today is not the day to sit around and wallow in the list of negativity and seemingly (yet not actually) awful realities associated with the title of *Miss*.

You know what wallowing does for you? It drowns you. It defeats you. It overwhelms you until you dig your head in the sand and raise the white flag. Quit doing the mental checklist of all the things you think are unfair about your life right now. I'm not saying that list isn't real life and doesn't have validity, but dwelling on those burdens won't do you any good.

Sure, your yard is a hot mess, your sink isn't draining quite right, you're vacillating on a decision that may relocate you far away, and best of all – that wasp nest on your porch is doing a mighty fine impression of an overpopulated pep-rally.

It is frustrating. I get it. And you're probably too tired to deal with your frustrations. I hear you and I feel you. The world tells you that you have two options. As previously mentioned, they are taking up camp on the "hanging in there and giving this single life your bravest of faces" side or sitting down, singing that song that cries "Woe is me" and thinking you have it worse than anyone else. But let me tell you something. Before you put your big-girl panties on and push through your frustration, or give up entirely and succumb to the self-depraved and self-pity era of your life, there is a better way. There is a way that the Lord has deemed worthy. You know what He calls us to?

*Honesty.* He calls us to honesty with Him. Not your Facebook friends or your Snapchat story. He calls you to be honest with Him.

There is absolutely no use faking strength, and it's all good to your Creator. He knows. He knows your heart better than you. He made it. He hears you before you say a word. He wants you to confess what you're feeling and what you're frustrated with. He wants your deepest, darkest secrets. He wants to hear your victories and your defeats. Tears don't stress Him out. Cry out to Him. Grab a tissue and get vulnerable with Jesus. He created you to need Him, talk to Him, and unload your burdens onto Him.

> Come to Me, all who are weary and heavy-laden, and I
> will give you rest. Take My yoke upon you and learn from
> Me, for I am gentle and humble in heart, and you will find
> rest for your souls. For My yoke is easy and My burden is
> light. (Matthew 11:28–30 NASB)

And in those moments, something beautiful will happen. He will talk back. He will pick up your broken pieces and start filling you with life. He will walk you through His scriptures and show you His strength, His might, His capability.

He will tell you that it is okay that you cannot do this single life well. He can and will pick up the slack. He will not tell you to be Wonder Woman. He will tell you to lean into Him as you move forward and sort through this haphazard season. Stop trying to go at it alone. It won't work.

Instead of feeling sorry for yourself, sit down at the feet of Jesus and listen to what He has to say to you. None of us is perfect, and there is no one right way to be a single girl. The world either idolizes it or shames those walking through it. It is time to walk that narrow road Jesus was talking about, and that includes your season of singleness.

Dear friend, I say all of this with purity and sincerity because I too have had to make the choice: giving up and complaining because I will never be able to hang a shower curtain rod, or surrendering this season to Jesus and letting Him dictate what my attitude should reflect (His grace) and what my daily purpose should look like (furthering His kingdom.)

So get your tissues and get alone with the God who longs to pick up your slack. Let Him in. You won't regret it.

> "Fear not, for you will not be put to shame; and do not
> feel humiliated, for you will not be disgraced; but you
> will forget the shame of your youth, and the reproach of
> your widowhood you will remember no more. For your

husband is your Maker, whose name is the Lord of hosts; and your Redeemer is the Holy One of Israel, who is called the God of all the earth. For the Lord has called you, like a wife forsaken and grieved in spirit, even like a wife of one's youth when she is rejected," says your God. "For a brief moment I forsook you, but with great compassion I will gather you. In an outburst of anger I hid My face from you for a moment, but with everlasting lovingkindness I will have compassion on you," says the Lord your Redeemer. (Isaiah 54:4-8 NASB)

# Motive

Dear Single Girl,

Today is a new day. This moment is brand-new. You can relax and praise God for mercy and fresh mornings that leave behind yesterday's mishaps and drudgery.

Think with me now. What defines you? What in your life makes you, you? Each day, what drives you to be who you are? What do you see yourself as?

Is it your job? Are you a teacher? A nurse? A retail saleswoman?

Is it your appearance? Are you blonde? Brunette? A ginger? Thick? Thin?

Is it your hobbies? Are you a traveler? A foodie? A runner? A cross-fitter? A reader?

Or is it your current relationship status? Are you happily single? Desperate? Looking?

There are so many ways to define yourself. There are so many external qualities and character traits that are able to label you in five words or less. When you think of yourself, or when others look at you, are you only motivated by those five words? Are you letting the stamp of *athleticism* or *striking beauty* dictate who you are?

Are the things you do on a day-to-day basis carried out to fit a status quo, or do you simply enjoy them?

Sister friend, I just want to chat for a quick second. First, I want to ask you your motive. Second, I want to tell you that you are enough.

The motive. Let's get to the nitty-gritty. Why do you eat the way you do? Why do you run all those miles? Why do you binge-watch thirty episodes of *Gilmore Girls*? Why do you binge-drink with your friends? Is it to have common ground with others, to fit in and attempt to find community? Is it to carry your head high and tote around the label of success? Do you push yourself so hard to fit a mold that the world considers worthy and desirable?

I am not asking all of these questions with an accusatory and judgmental pen. I am quietly asking you the same questions I ask myself. In this moment, be honest with yourself. Don't justify or give excuses. Examine your heart. If you find in that special heart of yours any motive that is not one to serve and glorify Jesus Christ, then it is time to kneel before the King. If you walk each day trying to be good enough for the world, you are serving both God and man. If you are making choices to catch the attraction and attention of man, you are betraying the divine romance established by and from the Lord.

> For am I now seeking the favor of men, or of God? Or am I striving to please men? If I were still trying to please men, I would not be a bond servant of Christ. (Galatians 1:10 NASB)

Hear me now and grasp what I am saying. You are a prized possession of the Lord as a born-again daughter of the King, Jesus, if you have accepted His salvation. You don't have to prove a thing to Him. You are enough to have and to hold His unswerving gaze. He sees down to the core of your spirit, the good with the bad. He will always choose you.

It doesn't matter how fast you can run a mile or how perfect your apple pie tastes. He loves you. He wants you to enjoy Him and the things of His kingdom more than the things sought after by the world. He wants your heart, and He wants your motives.

If you know your heart needs a tune-up and your motives need some TLC, it is okay. Mine do too. Everyone on this earth could use some sanctification. Praise God for His willingness to accomplish this with His power, not yours. Be honest with Him, and He will be ever faithful. I promise.

> Now may the God of peace Himself sanctify you entirely; and may your spirit and soul and body be preserved complete; without blame at the coming of our Lord Jesus Christ. Faithful is He who calls you, and He also will bring it to pass. (1 Thessalonians 5:23–24 NASB)

It takes time. It takes effort. It takes a huge dose of honesty with yourself and with the Lord to admit an impure motive. He already knows the root of your motives, but you must acknowledge and ask for help from Him. Purity cannot coexist with impurity. Light cannot coexist with darkness. Godliness cannot coexist with worldliness. Jesus came to rescue us from our impurities, our darkness, and our worldliness. He even came to rescue us from what appears to be innocent and harmless but in reality is stealing the abundant life the Cross offers us, a life redeemed from selfishness and godlessness. It is time to dig deep and see what the Lord is leading you to evaluate within yourself. He is forever in your corner, wanting what is best for you.

> For He rescued us from the domain of darkness, and transferred us to the kingdom of His beloved Son, in

whom we have redemption, the forgiveness of sins.
(Colossians 1:13–14 NASB)

Let us ask Him to redeem our motives today and reveal the deepest parts of our spirits that need fresh life. Oh, how able is He to meet us at our greatest need, even a need we didn't know we had. He won't leave a stone unturned. He won't leave you behind. His relentless love is real for you, my friend. Let Him win.

Instead of wearing the badge of worldly honor today, replace it with a bowing head and kneeling before the One who breathes worth and beauty into you. He gets the glory. He gets the credit. He is the Master Creator and Gift Giver.

> Not to us, O Lord, not to us, but to Your name give glory because of Your lovingkindness, because of Your truth.
> (Psalm 115:1 NASB)

# Settling

Dear Single Girl,

Come sit with me for just a second. I want to remind you of something today.

Has anyone ever told you that you're too picky? That your standards are way too high? That those type of guys do not exist? Or the best one, that you're just going to need to lower your standards?

Most of these comments were probably not said in a mean-spirited or discouraging way. You have people in your life who love you and care about you. They want you to be taken care of, happy, and in love. They want the best for you, and they are probably trying to help you out.

But step away from their good intentions turned sour remarks and hear this. It is not a bad thing to have high standards. You are not off base when you stay selective and picky in a culture where gentlemen are traded in for weak and passive boys. You should *never* feel ashamed for not settling.

The Lord calls His children to holiness and His perfect ways. No human in the flesh is capable of perfection, but Jesus has given us a standard by which to model our lives. And if someone is seeking the Lord with all her heart and soul and mind, this will overflow into all areas of her life, even dating. But let us set aside dating for a hot second.

In your life, you probably have been taught to do your best, strive for excellence, and never give up. Words ingrained within our minds. None of those goals is bad. But if Jesus hasn't infiltrated your motives or actions, most things will be done in vain. If His glory is not at the forefront of all you do, you will be spinning your wheels and tiring yourself. Jesus does in fact call us to be holy as He is holy, but by His strength and motivation. He will bring you to situations that are only able to be conquered by Him and with His high standard and excellence. You must surrender to Jesus every dark corner of your life and release the desire to be good and perfect on your own.

Now, let's get back to dating and marriage. I say to you, my sweet single girl, who has entertained the thought of lowering your standards because you don't think a godly man is going to come your way: Don't even think of settling for less than you deserve, less than what God has for you. I am looking at my fridge, and right in the middle is a piece of paper that says, "You're not the kind of girl who settles. Keep not settling."

Listen, sweet girl. I am assuming you hold yourself to a pretty high standard. You go through each day doing your best to please the Lord and enjoy your time on this earth. I'm praying you have a healthy self-esteem because you should. You are created in the image of God, and with Jesus, you are complete, beautiful, and worthy. You have so much going for you. With that being said, you don't lower your standards for yourself, so why would you do so for the man you want leading you?

It truly breaks my heart when girls settle for someone they think is a half winner when in reality they are full losers. Now, don't hear what I'm not saying; no one is perfect. We all have flaws—big ones. We are all, as believers, walking the path of sanctification. We are works in progress. There are just as many loser guys as loser girls out there. But when a man doesn't love and follow, and he doesn't let Jesus give him a heart after His own, then he isn't the one for you.

> Only conduct yourselves in a manner worthy of the gospel
> of Christ. (Philippians 1:27a NASB)

If he is not walking in a path that points his gaze and the eyes and hearts of those around him to Jesus, then his path is not intended for you. It is in your best interest to turn the other direction if the opportunity arises.

Again, don't hear what I'm not saying. There are petty things you could let go of from that list of yours. *At least this tall. This color hair. Has to have this amount of money.* Some things are superficial, and sister friend, we have to get past the superficial. We must get into the heart of the matter. Your standards for a man and his character should remain high. Raise that bar, and raise it proudly.

Why would you settle for an opportunity that could be an open door from the enemy, intended to derail you and pull you away from your Father's heart? Why would you do that when you could sit down, wait on the Lord with hope, and know He has big plans and bright tomorrows for you? I am not just blowing air here—I believe this with all my heart.

> And we know that God causes all things to work together
> for good to those who love God, to those who are called
> according to His purpose. (Romans 8:28 NASB)

It's so much better to be picky than to end up attached to a man who doesn't know how to endure inevitable hard times because his entire trust is not in the Lord.

So, my single girl, the next time you feel as though you're the only one with high standards, know this: you are, in fact, in the presence of your King, the God of high standards, holy living, and grace.

# *Post Script*

Now for a little transparency. This letter was written prior to the season of my life where suffering held hands with abundant life, where loss made friends with deep joy, where my emotions were on overdrive and mixed with espresso. I smile as I come back to these words, and I would like to offer a little hindsight from experience to this letter.

With regard to falling for a scheme from the enemy that could snatch you away from your Father's heart, I was just there. I catch my breath because this could have been me. Friend, this was almost me. I was a girl walking through a door with clouded emotions and grief in her heart, leaning on a man who did not intend to hold a permanent place in my story. This is a story for another day, but the lessons and faithfulness of my Jesus are so deeply real, so deeply learned, and so deeply appreciated.

We were never intended to walk this life without wise counsel. We were never intended to settle for what looks good on paper but holds unrest in our spirits. We were never intended to think logically instead of using divine discernment. We were never intended to walk dictated by our emotions.

Jesus uses people of truth to speak blessings, counsel, and life into us. Listen to them instead of listening to your feelings. I know you have a lot of them, and so do I. Our feelings have to get put on the sideline when life gets real. Listen to the people who know Jesus, live well with Jesus, and have a lot of life with Jesus under their belts. Be careful not to listen to the people who say only what you want to hear. Remember, Jesus only tells the truth and often is not warm and fuzzy—or what our flesh wants.

> Without consultation, plans are frustrated, but with many counselors they succeed. (Proverbs 15:22 NASB)

You know that uneasiness, the red flags you feel but want to ignore? Jesus gives us these checks in our spirits for a reason. It is the Holy Spirit who lives within us guiding us to holiness. Listen to Him. If it doesn't line up with scripture or the Lord's prompting, then it isn't right. Plain and simple.

Jesus makes the logic of this world seem foolish and turns the heads of most people. He is going to operate within His character in your personal life, too. When He says wait when the world around you says go, please wait.

> My soul waits in silence for God only; from Him is my salvation. (Psalm 62:1 NASB)

Jesus does not want us to overthink big decisions or even small ones. He calls us to rely on Him for direction. Pray about it; don't analyze it. Listen to His truth and go with it.

Sister, I wish we could go get coffee so you could see my face and hear how much I mean all of this and how close this is to my heart. I was close to being that girl who settles for something half good because there is an opportunity for marriage. Jesus rescued me from a story that would have ended in darkness, heartache, and loneliness. It would have been an ending of shame the enemy wanted to be able to sing over me. But now Jesus will continue to sing songs of deliverance over me, and He wants to do the same for you.

> Blessed be the Lord, who daily bears our burden, the God who is our salvation. God is to us a God of deliverances; and to God the Lord belong escapes from death. (Psalm 68:19–20 NASB)

That is why I write to you. I pray wherever you are in your story, Jesus will be the victor. I pray that He will rescue you from settling, from desperation, from the "what could have beens." He did for me what I asked of Him: to protect me and keep me. Even with a little wear and tear, I still have life, I still have hope, and I still have my Jesus.

> Blessed be God, who has not turned away my prayer nor His lovingkindness from me. (Psalm 66:20 NASB)

# You Have
# Permission to Give Up

Dear Single Girl,

Come sit with me for a moment. Come listen to what the Father has to say to your heart. He has been investing a lot of time into me this weekend, and I want you to be encouraged with what He told me.

I have a question. Since when did it become shameful and distasteful to give up? When you hear that someone gave up, either you turn your nose in the air in arrogance, or you have pity on that unsuccessful soul. *She didn't try hard enough. She couldn't do it. She failed miserably.* Those are things I have said and thought.

The lady bosses and independent women of the world have infiltrated our lives and churches. In doing so, this headstrong, tough, and hard generation of females (not ladies) has emerged. These females don't wear their emotions on their sleeves. They don't want babies. They overpower men and forsake femininity.

The feminist movement has gone too far and is eerily reminiscent of Queen Jezebel. This queen ruled her household and did not submit to her husband, who was the king of Israel.

The queen was godless, manipulative, and crass. She caused a mighty man of God to flee her presence—not just walk away. Elijah "ran for his life" (1 Kings 19:3 NASB).

> Surely there was no one like Ahab who sold himself to do evil in the sight of the LORD, because Jezebel his wife incited him. (1 Kings 21:25 NASB)

Wouldn't you like that to be written on your tombstone? You influenced your husband to bear the banner of opposer to the Most High God? No thanks.

When Ahab married Jezebel, he went to serve Baal and worship him.

> It came about, as though it had been a trivial thing for him to walk in the sins of Jeroboam the son of Nebat, that he married Jezebel the daughter of Ethbaal king of the Sidonians, and went to serve Baal and worshiped him. (1 Kings 16:31 NASB)

One commentary in the NASB Study Bible says, "Omri's son Ahab married Ethbaal's daughter to seal the alliance [and] led to widespread Baal worship in the Northern Kingdom and eventually to the near extinction of the Davidic line in the Southern Kingdom."

If you've read the story of Ahab before, you know he isn't the first king to carry out the sins of his father or do evil in the sight of the Lord. But the fact that a woman now has a shout-out to being the big hinge on which great evil and idol worship rest on is a big deal. You see, this non-Israelite lady did not fit into or mold into the role of a wife designed by the Lord. She was unwilling to serve the Lord or turn from her idols and cursed ways. As they say, it takes two to tango, and she is not fully to blame. A marriage is between two people, and passive, walked-all-over Ahab is at fault as well. But right now, I want us to focus on the hard-hearted lady.

You may be thinking, *This woman sounds awful.* But she was capable. She was smart. She knew her way around a man's business room (her husband's kingdom). She was in no need of help. She sounds like a present-day woman—the woman who rises high in the corporate world; the woman who works while her husband stays home; the woman who never gives up.

But you know what was said of Queen Jezebel?

> The dogs will eat Jezebel in the district of Jezreel. (1 Kings 21:23b NASB)

A man didn't say this—God did. The Lord spoke those words over her. May it never be said of me, by God, that I will be a late-night snack for some dog. Get me as far away from that as possible.

Now listen, beloved. Don't hear what I'm not saying. The Lord does in fact tell us to be strong and to not lose heart, which the Queen did well in doing. But her flaw? She let her strength, her intellect, and her success all come from within herself. *She* was the endurance. *She* was the capable one. *She* was the brains of the operations. Not only was she the brains, but she was the driving force. She used whatever it took to be in charge over Ahab.

And this, my friend, is not the role God intended for a wife. It is as if she despised being behind the scenes, being subject to a man, and being out of control. She could not stand being in the backseat. She played on the weakness of Ahab's passivity and lack of leadership and ran him out of the driver's seat. Instead of encouraging and supporting, she took away any ounce of self-respect and pride her man may have had. The curse upon her was obvious, and the enemy used her in his ploy to tear down not only their family but also part of the Israelite kingdom. In doing so, this backward marriage walked far from God with blinded eyes and wounded souls.

Oh, how we are all capable of walking in a manner such as Jezebel. We may walk with fierce determination. We may walk proudly while forsaking tending to the needs of others. We may walk at a pace that sees to our own wants and won't stop until they have been accomplished. I will be the first to admit that I have been there. I have been that woman who thought she had it all together, who thought I could coast through this life without any vulnerability showing on that pink floral sleeve of mine. I thought I could operate perfectly on the same level as the thick-skinned and successful corporate Americans out there.

One of the roles I have in my day job is the role of an administrative supervisor, white jacket and all. While training for the transition into this role with authority, I thought, *I've got this. I will act confident and not let everyone see how unprepared and underqualified I feel to wear this white jacket and carry these two phones.*

Wrong. The vulnerability cannot be hidden when you are thrown into a situation that is completely foreign and downright frightening, and when all eyes look to you for the answer. When lives are on the line, death is such a real possibility for patients, and you watch a family watch their child take his or her last breath, you cannot fake being unaffected by real life suffering and loss. Fake confidence shatters; enter the genuine need to learn and grow.

My mind-set was immediately shifted before I officially held that title because I realized how little capability and knowledge I had on my own. How quickly I was humbled in the midst of situations that rightly warranted asking for help and admitting I needed assistance, guidance, and the option to phone a friend for help.

Friend, Jezebel forgot she was human. She forgot she didn't know everything. She forgot she had limitations. She forgot there was more to life than the appearance of having it all together. She also never sought the Lord. She never called upon Him for help. She never gave up. She never once came to the end of herself and cried out to the King of kings and said, "I surrender, Lord. My heart is overwhelmed. I cannot make it one more step on my own. I give up."

Does this sound like you, sweet sister? Does this queen who is remembered only for her negative contributions to God's people and her marriage have any similarities to your heart? If you are kin to this mind-set and heart attitude, welcome to the club. Welcome to real life and a need for grace and new life in Christ. Of course, you have something in common with this godless lady; we all do. And we all need His help in overcoming any remnant of this disgrace in our lives.

When we choose to give up and cry to Him, His response is magnificently simple. He says, "I AM able." Not that I, Alyssa, am able. He says, "I AM able." The great I AM. He is the only one able. He is the only one capable. He has perfect strength and perfect endurance. He fills our weary and empty cups with Himself. In our giving up, He rises up within us to keep us going, to win, to fight, to accomplish what's before us. It's by His grace, not ours.

> For by grace you have been saved through faith; and that not of yourselves, it is the gift of God; not as a result of works, so that no one may boast. (Ephesians 2:8–9 NASB)

Sister friend, stop being strong. Stop reigning in your own life. You're exhausted because you were never designed to hold the burdens of your life on your tired, sweet shoulders. Stop being your own savior because it doesn't work. Trust me.

Give up. Kneel down today with open hands and give up the control to the King who loves you. I am praying for you. I know it is a big deal. Let go and trust in the One who paints the sunsets and breathes melodies from the winds. He is able.

> But He gives a greater grace. Therefore it says, "God is opposed to the proud, but gives grace to the humble." Submit therefore to God. Resist the devil and he will flee from you. Draw near to God and He will draw near to you. Cleanse your hands, you sinners; and purify your hearts, you double-minded. (James 4:6–8 NASB)

And through giving up, I trust He is going to revive a generation of ladies that resembles the original intent for His female design: a God-fearing, warm-hearted, quietly capable servant who uplifts those around her by grace. Lord, let me be this type of lady. Until my title changes from *Miss* to *Mrs.*, allow me to walk in the lane You have prepared for me with the grace given to me at the Cross. That grace will push me to walk with the designed characteristics You give to all of Your daughters. I want to live out what Proverbs 31:25 says: "strength and dignity are her clothing, and she smiles at the future," with the Cross in my gaze. That gaze is so humbled by Your hope that when it is time for a change of season, welcomed with a man to lead, my heart cry would still cling to You more than the long-awaited promise of a husband. Lord, let us all be this type of lady.

This type of lady lets You mold her into a wife who operates in her role. She is united with a redeemed man who is confident in his leadership, authority, and decision making. This type of man does not mindlessly dictate but humbly leads and serves with the support of a capable woman. The woman stays in her lane, respects Godly male leadership, and joyfully serves her family (and ultimately the Lord) in every action, motive, and prayer for the rest of her days. Break the curses of Jezebel in our hearts and land, Lord. Be big.

> Older women likewise are to be reverent in their behavior, not malicious gossips nor enslaved to much wine, teaching what is good, so that they may encourage the young women to love their husbands, to love their children, to be sensible, pure, workers at home, kind, being subject to their own husbands, so that the word of God will not be dishonored. (Titus 2:3–5 NASB)

# Come to Me

Dear Single Girl,

Are you having a hard time right now? Are you in the midst of a storm-tossed season? Have the circumstances around you become overwhelming and engulfing? Come sit with me and with Jesus. Let the burdens be pushed aside for a few moments. Let the emotions be set down and the tears be quieted.

Sweet girl, this life is hard. This life we live can be crazy one minute and calm the next. Struggles and trials plague each and every one of us. None of us is immune to sorrow, suffering, or sadness. I don't know your personal grief right now, but I know it is so deep and real. Is the pain that makes you want to just sit down and give up, the pain that doesn't make sense and won't ease up, still fresh? You're walking in the thick of it, aren't you? And on top of this pain comes the burden of walking through this without a man at your side to pick up some of the slack.

If this is you, and this rough season is getting to you, listen to what Jesus has been telling me. And if this isn't you, please listen anyway. This could have already been you, or it will be you, or you could share this with a fellow sister friend to help her broken heart.

My daughter, come to Me. Come as you are right now. Your gaze has been focused on the storm outside your window. Your eyes are looking through the lens of the world to dwell on the pain, the loss, the confusion, and the unfairness. You're overcome with sorrow.

Come to Me.

Step away from the window and come bow down your weary shoulders before Me. Let your hands release the weight of the stress and control of this situation. I know you can hear the wind raging and the powerful thunder trying to overtake you, but My beloved, listen to Me.

This situation and season did not surprise Me. I knew it was on the horizon and saw it coming. I know in your mind's eye the logic of this tragedy doesn't make sense, but you must keep trusting Me. Stop limiting My ability by your ability. I made you. I breathe life into you every day. I am your beginning and your end. This world is filled with trouble. My heart is grieved by this trouble. That is why this earth is not your home. Your home is with Me in glory. I came to save you to give you new life now and a forever home free of sorrow, free of suffering, and free of tears. The sin that plagues this world and my children is inescapable while you are still a fleshly body. I give you tools to lead an abundant life and to walk free from the deep sin from within. The external circumstances will always be laced with trials.

Your life is but a breath, and soon you will be with Me in glory. But until then, come to Me. Dig deep into My Word and find truth there. Hear Me speak to your burdened heart through My scriptures. I am right here. I am within you. I am sitting right next to you, mourning with you. Allow Me to bear this weight. You simply cannot. I can.

Let Me show you how to live each day with grace, joy, and dignity. It isn't easy, but it is possible. You must see Me above all else. Your gaze must remain upon Me. When you lose sight of Me, your step will slip, and the weight of what's going on around you will drag you to the depths of despair. Each day I will give you a word of truth. Just come to Me.

Don't make sense of it. Come to Me.

When the doctor says cancer, come to Me.

When the funeral is over, come to Me.

When you're sitting on your living room floor and at a loss for how to live, come to Me.

When it just isn't fair, come to Me.

I know the man I have for you has not arrived to the party yet. I am all you need right now and forever. He cannot fix this or mend your heart, only I can. I know exactly what you need. You need Me.

Don't feel sorry for yourself. Each woman is walking in her own version of a battle. Let Me use you to be a light and a joy. You have Me within you. All else in your life is a want, not a need.

And my God will supply all your needs according to His riches in glory in Christ Jesus. (Philippians 4:19 NASB)

Sorrow isn't new. I promise you will be able to breathe if you let Me in. Come to Me.

This is a glimpse of what my Jesus has been preaching to me. Each day, rise to meet the one who loves your more than life itself. Let Him mend your heart. Be honest with Him. Let Him speak back to you. Listen patiently, sister. He always answers.

Surely our griefs He Himself bore, and our sorrows He carried; yet we ourselves esteemed Him stricken, smitten of God, and afflicted. But He was pierced through for our transgressions, He was crushed for our iniquities; the chastening for our well-being fell upon Him, and by His scourging we are healed. All of us like sheep have gone astray, each of us has turned to his own way; but the Lord has caused the iniquity of us all to fall on Him. (Isaiah 53:4–6 NASB)

"Shout for joy, O barren one, you who have borne no child; break forth into joyful shouting and cry aloud, you who have not travailed; for the sons of the desolate one will be more numerous than the sons of the married woman," says the Lord.

"Enlarge the place of your tent; stretch out the curtains of your dwellings, spare not; lengthen your cords and strengthen your pegs. For you will spread abroad to the right and to the left. And your descendants will possess nations and will resettle the desolate cities. Fear not, for you will not be put to shame; and do not feel humiliated, for you will not be disgraced; but you will forget the shame of your youth, and the reproach of your widowhood you will remember no more. For your husband is your Maker whose name is the Lord of Hosts; and your Redeemer is the Holy One of Israel, who is called the God of all the earth. For the Lord has called you, like a wife forsaken and grieved in spirit, even like a wife of one's youth when she is rejected," says your God.

"For a brief moment I forsook you, but with great compassion I will gather you. In an outburst of anger I hid My face from you for a moment, but with everlasting lovingkindness I will have compassion on you," says the Lord your Redeemer.

"For this is like the days of Noah to Me, when I swore that the waters of Noah would not flood the earth again; so I have sworn that I will not be angry with you nor will I rebuke you. For the mountains may be removed and the hills may shake, but My lovingkindness will not be removed from you, and My covenant of peace will not be shaken," says the Lord who has compassion on you.

"O afflicted one, storm-tossed, and not comforted, behold, I will set your stones in antimony, and your foundations I will lay in sapphires. Moreover, I will make your battlements of rubies, and your gates of crystal, and your entire wall of precious stones. All your sons will be taught of the Lord; and the well-being of your sons will be great. In righteousness you will be established; you will be far from oppression, for you will not fear; and from terror, for it will not come near you. If anyone fiercely assails you it will not be from Me. Whoever assails you will fall because of you. Behold, I Myself have created the smith who blows the fire of coals and brings out a weapon for its work; and I have created the destroyer to ruin. No weapon that is formed against you will prosper; and every tongue that accuses you in judgement you will condemn. This is the heritage of the servants of the Lord, and their vindication is from Me," declares the Lord."
(Isaiah 54 NASB)

# *Only Jesus*

Dear Single Girl,

How is your precious soul today? Are you having a good day, a day where your hair did what it was supposed to do and your eyeliner is straight? Or are you having a *big sigh* kind of day, a day where everyone else's grass looks greener?

Well, turn off social media for a moment. Let the beautiful, filtered, and staged pictures of everyone else flee your mind. Come sit with me and let the Lord sweetly lift your face. He tells us and promises us with sound faithfulness that "They looked to Him and were radiant, and their faces will never be ashamed" (Psalm 34:5 NASB).

Hear the finality and beauty of His sweet promise in that verse. *Never be ashamed*. Never. *Never* is such a strong word. I tend to not use that word too often in my life because more often than not, I eat my words when I say never. *I will never be a nurse. I will never buy a house until I am married. I will never run a marathon. I will never mow my own yard.*

Reality check. Sister, I *am* a nurse. I own my home. I *did* run a marathon. I *do* mow my grass (sometimes). In my ignorance and defiance, I crossed my arms and pursed my lips as I shook my head at my Savior and said, "No way" to all of those things. I had no desire for any of them. And believe me, there are many more instances where I'm pretty sure Jesus chuckled at my insistence of never doing this or that. Basically, I told Him that I was not willing to be flexible and surrender to His ways and go wherever He led me, even if it was not on my radar or agenda.

But through some refining, some dying to my desires, and some (well quite a lot of) tears, here I am. I'm a girl who has a mortgage, wears scrubs a few times a week, runs some miles here and there, and knows how to start a lawnmower. All of this was ordained and initiated by Jesus, even when I said never. Because clearly I could forecast my future and see what was best for me.

Because I shy away from the word *never*, I am usually all ears when I read it in scripture. The only one who can use that word with 100 percent authority is Jesus, the one who sees all, is all, and orchestrates all. Only He can speak it and *mean it*.

Here, He tells us that those who look to Him will *never* be ashamed. Never. Never be ashamed. And not only will you never be ashamed, but you'll be radiant. That is a fully loaded statement. Add some bacon and cheese, and that fully loaded plate of truth could be the party of the year. No shame. *And* radiance?

Lord, are You sure that's what You mean? Are You sure You mean it? Because that hefty verse could change this culture's entire way of thinking.

Oh, what's that, Lord? Oh, right. You are the Alpha and Omega. The one who is life. The God of redemption and grace. The Jesus who has all authority. The only one who holds the confidence and sovereignty of Scripture. The Savior who always means what He says and never speaks out of turn. Only Jesus.

Okay, so He means it. He means it when He says we will be

radiant and never be ashamed. He rewards His needy children with Himself, with Jesus.

His radiance and His glory. The antonyms of shame are honor and glory. Oh, how sweet to wear the crowns of radiance, glory, and honor. To stand in the face of fear and sadness and simply say, "Sorry, my Jesus placed His crown on me. The fully loaded crown of radiance, glory, and honor. Shame is not a part of me because it is not generated from my Jesus."

Rise in the oppressive confusion and let His radiance surround you and be within you, reaching the nooks and crannies of your weary soul and going all the way into the smoky circumstance all around you. Only Jesus can do that. Only Jesus can be your overcomer.

> But in all these things we overwhelmingly conquer through Him who loved us. (Romans 8:37 NASB)

Only Jesus can rewire your mind from one of defeat and guilt into one of hope, victory, and triumph.

> For God has not given us a spirit of timidity, but of power and love and discipline. (2 Timothy 1:7 NASB)

Only Jesus can silence the voices of the enemy that attack your insecurities.

> We are destroying speculations and every lofty thing raised up against the knowledge of God, and we are taking every thought captive to the obedience of Christ. (2 Corinthians 10:5 NASB)

Only He can silence the lies that tickle your ears and push you to listen to the world instead of standing on the fully loaded promises of Jesus.

> Finally, be strong in the Lord and in the strength of His
> might. Put on the full armor of God, so that you will
> be able to stand firm against the schemes of the devil.
> (Ephesians 6:10–11 NASB)

Sister friend, only Jesus. Hear me now. When you desperately and truly cry out to Jesus, He will hear you. He will show you areas of darkness and strongholds of despair that *can* be defeated and redeemed. Only Jesus.

If you want to stop thinking shameful and defeated thoughts about yourself, ask Him to show you what caused those thoughts. Ask Him to show you His truths about who you are in Christ, not who you once were. He will be faithful. The battle is real when it comes to living a radiant life. Seek Him and seek fellow faithful believers to walk alongside of you on your road to radiance. Let those who have gone before you come next to you and confidently say, "Only Jesus."

Know, sweet girl, that just because you aren't married, this is not cause for shame. Just because you also mow your grass, there is no shame. Just because you get carryout on Friday nights and eat on your couch while reading a book or watching a movie, there is no shame. And just because you are choosing Jesus over another dead-end guy, there is absolutely no shame in choosing the road to radiance.

Don't let the lies of the enemy fill you with shame for placing your stake in the ground for the worthy road. You grab your sword, turn to Psalm 34, and proclaim to the enemy those truths. Remind him, and remind yourself who the real victor is. Remind him of the radiance. Read all the way from verse 1 to verse 22. Remind him the True Deliverer has him beat. Only Jesus.

> I will bless the Lord at all times; His praise shall continually
> be in my mouth. My soul will make its boast in the Lord;

the humble will hear it and rejoice. O magnify the Lord with me, and let us exalt His name together.

I sought the Lord, and He answered me, and delivered me from all my fears. They looked to Him and were radiant, and their faces will never be ashamed. This poor man cried, and the Lord heard him and saved him out of all his troubles. The angel of the Lord encamps around those who fear Him, and rescues them.

O taste and see that the Lord is good; how blessed is the man who takes refuge in Him! O fear the Lord, you His saints; for to those who fear Him there is no want. The young lions do lack and suffer hunger; but they who see the Lord shall not be in want of any good thing.

Come, you children, listen to me; I will teach you the fear of the Lord. Who is the man who desires life and loves length of days that he may see good? Keep your tongue from evil and your lips from speaking deceit. Depart from evil and do good; seek peace and pursue it.

The eyes of the Lord are toward the righteous and His ears are open to their cry. The face of the Lord is against evildoers, to cut off the memory of them from the earth.

The righteous cry, and the Lord hears and delivers them out of all their troubles. The Lord is near to the brokenhearted and saves those who are crushed in spirit. Many are the afflictions of the righteous, but the Lord delivers him out of them all. He keeps all his bones, not one of them is broken.

Evil shall slay the wicked, and those who hate the righteous will be condemned. The Lord redeems the soul of His servants, and none of those who take refuge in Him will be condemned. (Psalm 34 NASB)

# The Storms Are Rough Sometimes

Dear Single Girl,

Are there things in your life that you wish were different? Are there issues with your family that are doing their best to discourage you? Do you feel as though you can't catch a break and that each corner you turn hits you with a large, flashing sign of overwhelming burden?

Can I tell you a secret? Me too.

Life can have some pretty rocky roads and stormy seas. I wanted to open up to you a little in this letter to show you where I'm coming from when I write to you. I want you to feel a sense of camaraderie with this single girl with a real life who loves real talk.

Today is Saturday, and I finally have a weekend off work. This weekend warrior loves being a nurse on the weekends, but I also love a nice, relaxing Saturday that isn't filled with someone else's body fluids, sick kids, or hospital drama. And on this Saturday off, I have decided to put on my big-girl panties and take care of a pressing need in my sweet and cozy home.

Spiders.

*I hate spiders. Oh, I really don't like them, Jesus. Can You please rid my house of them? I just can't. Jesus, I can't. Oh ... shoot. There's another spider.*

These thoughts and prayers were the base of my discussion I was having with the Lord in my pajamas as I held the multigallon jug of bug spray and sprayed the inside perimeter of my house.

Sister, I just can't with spiders. And because the weather is warmer, I've seen *too many* inside of my house. Panic rises within my generally calm spirit, and uncharacteristic expletives are suddenly at the tip of my tongue when I come across those eight-legged arachnids. Spiders inside and outside of my house on my property, my safe place, is something I wish was different. I'm pretty sure the fact that I keep seeing them means that Jesus has a sense of humor. Now, I know what you're thinking: spiders are surely not what are causing some stress in my life at the moment. Okay, fine, they're not the biggest thing. They are just spiders after all. No, this is not the biggest thing I wish was different about this season of my life.

Today marks three months since my mom was diagnosed with stage four lung cancer. In these three months, so much has happened. My heart has been squeezed ever so tightly. There are many stories for another time and another letter. But, sister, do you have someone in your life who is sick? Are you watching someone you love so dearly suffer? I am walking this difficult road with you. If you have already walked that achy path, I am so very sorry for your pain and overwhelming grief.

I want you to know that I too have circumstances that are not ideal. And that is just one of them; the ones in the past have stories too, but again, another time in another letter.

The people around you have stories just like you. Maybe your car won't start today. Maybe you and a coworker are at odds, and your once enjoyable environment has now become laced with tension and stress ulcers. Maybe there isn't enough money in that checking account of yours to make ends meet. And to top it off, you're facing these hurdles without a man at your side.

There are so many things that are difficult, unwelcome, and downright frustrating. I know, sweet girl, that it feels like this life is trying to knock you down. The red boxing gloves of the enemy are extra strong right now and just landed a staggering right hook to that beautiful jaw of yours.

Want to know something? The enemy is trying to knock you out. He is doing his best to frustrate you. He has some pretty ugly plans for your life and for my life. His accusatory voice wants you and me to believe that we are isolated and must walk this life alone. He wants us to think that our circumstances, especially the bad ones, will overcome us and get us down for the count. One of his goals is to put our focus on the storm and grief it brings. He wants us to dwell on the negative, sulk in the sorrow, and take on the role of lonely victims.

His plan has not changed through the ages. The enemy isn't the most creative or original when it comes to organizing and planning missions to infiltrate our stability and faith. He eerily calls us to let our gaze remain focused on the devastation, to look on our trials with defeat and hopelessness. He wants the temporary and circumstantial to take center stage while overshadowing the eternal and holy implications of this uphill climb of a season. His goal is simple: to steal our peace that Jesus gives us and to deceive us into confusion, despair, and depression.

If you have never read Job in the Old Testament, and you're walking through an uncharacteristically challenging trial, you might want to get to know this man. No, it's not going to make you warm and fuzzy and give you the uplifting encouragement you might want. But it will open your eyes to the rawness of loss, the realities of unfair circumstances, and the expectation a redeemed believer in Jesus is held to when face-to-face with an attack or storm in his or her life. It's not for the weary in heart. I'm not going to spend a lot of time discussing Job, but I will share what this brutal section of scripture has taught me.

This successful man lived a life that most envied. He had the blessing of a large family, all the livestock his land needed, a life devoted to the Lord, and a heart that feared God. He appeared to balance the earthly success with appropriate reverence to his God. Thumbs-up for Job. God was in his corner; He commended Job for his holiness and piety. He blessed him, protected him, and clearly loved him.

And then a mighty disaster knocked on Job's door. He lost his physical possessions and his children all in one day. The apples of his eye were taken so quickly. His life changed without warning. His earthly security robbed every so quickly.

Do you know what Job's first words were in response to this grave news? I'll give you a hint: it is not what I expected, or what my response has been in trying times. Job worshipped God. He fell on his face and, despite the tears in his eyes and grief in his heart, blessed his King.

> Then Job arose and tore his robe and shaved his head, and he fell to the ground and worshiped. He said, "Naked I came from my mother's womb, and naked I shall return there. The Lord gave and the Lord has taken away. Blessed be the name of the Lord." Through all this Job did not sin nor did he blame God. (Job 1:20–22 NASB)

In his pain and loss, Job did not lose sight of the fact that God reigns supreme and executes beautiful sovereignty on His creation. I'm going to need a minute here. Every time I come to this paragraph in my Word, I have to take a pause. This man was robbed of his kids and his livestock. He lost his livelihood. Sure, a camel can be replaced, but a child?

Job looked past that. He turned his gaze to the one who held his heart. How can he do that? How can he bless Him when his heart should be torn to shreds? I've concluded the only way this is possible—and I mean the *only* way—is through grace. The grace of God instilled in him to have the audacity to lift his head and lock eyes with his Maker and Creator. Job had the Lord give him an unusual response, an unusual heart cry, and an unusual perspective in comparison to the world around him and what it was used to seeing.

"Oh, did you hear about poor Job of Uz? His livelihood, livestock, and children were all taken from him. And you know what that crazy guy did? He blessed God! Can you believe it? Crazy guy, that Job."

Crazy sounds about right to those who have lost eternal perspective and let the intent of the enemy overrule the truth of the Lord.

In Job's first response to tragedy, he continued to operate in submission to the awe-inspiring, mighty Warrior, the ever-loving King. Oh, how I need to be given a dose of Job's grit and endurance.

Now, there is a lot more to Job's story, and as life goes, he had to wrestle with his new realities and have some not-so-comfortable heart-to-heart talks with some friends and the Lord. Not all of his responses held the same tone of worship or the right way, *the holy way*, to speak to God. But in doing so, he was unapologetically honest, and we readers are able to feel his pain, understand his frustration, and see ourselves in his responses. We can see the pity and not the big picture but the here and now. We see how much we *don't* know compared to the High King. It's raw, honest, and tension filled. But it walks us through turmoil and despair and ends with newfound worship and reverence yet again.

> Then Job answered the Lord and said, "I know that
> You can do all things, and that no purpose of Yours can
> be thwarted." 'Who is this that hides counsel without
> knowledge?' "Therefore I have declared that which I did
> not understand, things too wonderful for me, which I did
> not know." 'Hear, now, and I will speak; I will ask You, and
> You instruct me.' "I have heard of You by the hearing of
> the ear; but now my eye sees You; therefore I retract, and
> I repent in dust and ashes." (Job 42:1–6 NASB)

The Lord allowed him to realize that He alone is able. He has His own agenda, all out of love for His children to know Him more. He has grace upon grace. He opened Job's eyes, let him truly comprehend his rightful place, and freed him from dwelling on the temporary hopelessness. Job was able to understand that life wasn't perfect or without pain, and the only one who remains constant and worth seeking is the same God who not only gives but takes away. When something is taken away, He is right there, ready to fill that wound, void, or broken heart with the lifeblood and everlasting peace that baffles this world.

> And the peace of God which surpasses all comprehension,
> will guard your hearts and your minds in Christ Jesus.
> (Philippians 4:7 NASB)

By allowing Jesus to give you this mind-set, you'd better believe the enemy's plans have been thwarted. No, it isn't easy. No, it isn't glamorous. No, it won't bring back what was lost. But your heart will be whole, and your joy will be revived.

When we, as grieving single girls, look beyond what is constricting our hearts, and when we fall to our knees and cry out in raw honesty to our Jesus. There He will be, ready to give us Himself, give us new life, give us hope, give us unworldly perspective, and give us a pure heart that will be able to truly say, "Come what may, but my hope stays on Jesus and my heart is one with Him. Blessed be the name of the Lord."

> As for you, you meant evil against me, but God meant it for good in order to bring about this present result, to preserve many people alive. (Genesis 50:20 NASB)

# Post Script

As previously discussed, this letter was written in the midst of my mom's journey with lung cancer. It's a story that, from the outside looking in, is one that many want to shy away from due to the raw pain that accompanies a grim diagnosis such as hers. This is not that letter for a different day to expand on that season, but this is a follow-up piece to part of my story.

If I were to timeline the last few years of my life, it would appear that I have jumped from the next rainy day to the next stormy month without much reprieve. One hard storm continued to hang around my family and me. Friend, my eyes rarely met a day when they were not filled with tears. Never once did I buy waterproof mascara—rookie mistake.

All joking aside, the facts in this chapter of my story are bleak. Yes, they are facts, but they are not the meat or the depth that bring life into the entire book written about my life. The details tucked away behind the circumstances that were not asked for are where Jesus can be found and shared.

Fact: My mom passed away after ten months of sickness.

Detail: My mom surrendered her heart to the Lord the last month she was alive and met her Savior that early morning in January.

Fact: My sister gave birth to her third baby without my mom on this side of heaven.

Detail: Jesus met her every need and loss with His grace and provision, even through tears.

Fact: I miss my mom on snowy winter days like today, because she loved them so deeply.

Detail: She is home with the Giver of snow, and she and I are both in awe of His beauty and wonder, as well as at His throne in worship.

The facts will always be facts. Those will not change. But the details ... Jesus gives me more of those every day that transform the facts He has given me into personal testimonies of His salvation, healing, power, and glory. In the tear-stained facts of my life, the Author of this life has graciously allowed me to know Him more and in new ways with every turn. I wouldn't trade them. I wouldn't rewrite them. I would simply ask that they keep shining His light to the darkness in which this world finds itself.

My sweet friend, you have your own facts. You have your own details that were born in the midst of pain. You may be trekking through a bleak season as you read these letters. My prayer for you is that, like Job, your heart will learn to seek the Lord first. Your first response would be one that praises God for His presence, even when every other ounce of hope seems lost. When the circumstantial good that what once was is quickly stripped from you, may your soul humbly bow before the God who meets every need, the God who is joy himself, the God who saves you from despair, the God who is the Creator of painted sunsets as well as a torrential downpour of rain. Like my cute dishtowel says in my kitchen, "No rain, no flowers."

May you and I both endure well in the rain. And when it ends, may we both arise stronger, wiser, and deeply in love with the Savior of this world.

# To Genuinely Know Him

Dear Single Girl,

First, I want you to know that I'm proud of you. You're walking a road that is as beautiful as it is frustrating. You have been carefully chosen to live this life in a unique way designed by the Master Planner.

He has not made this decision in haste. He wants you right here. He wants you facing your days with Him by your side. He wants you to sojourn through the oasis and even the desert. You may be unaware as to how you will survive the days that can occasionally be scorching and soul emptying. He specifically intended for you to enter into solitude, embrace the quiet home you inhabit, and be nourished by the encouragement of your perfect Bridegroom.

Hear Him as He calls you His bride and His beloved. His intense love and desire for your heart reigns supreme within His plan for your life. In the midst of the aching heart and tear-stained face that accompanies you, He is sitting with you and opening His heart to you. He isn't put off by your emotions, and neither does He shy away from the devastatingly honest cries, pleas, and questions that arise from your pain. He is ever so ready to open your eyes to His goodness, His faithfulness, and His divine purpose for you.

You were made for such a time as this. Sure, you may not be in a position to help save your family, friends, or entire nation, but you *were* made for this exact season, whether it be post-engagement without a wedding band but full of crushed hopes and dreams, or a job that requires your heart and your time while lacking a man to pick up your slack. Or maybe you're a mama who is husbandless yet manages to run a household solo without any precious time for yourself. You could be pre-engagement, never married, and you have not yet had that true love that apparently cures all ailments. You're just a girl walking bravely alone day to day.

However you fit in to the equation, at times you feel up to your eyeballs in less than desirable circumstances. At the end of your long days and exhausting weeks, you sink into your bed and whisper, "Why? Why, Lord? Why must it be this way?"

The end of this dreary season is nowhere in sight. The help has not seemed to come yet. Your shoulders are killing you from the weighty burdens that surround you. In these moments of giving up and despondency toward your sweet and trying life, Jesus has something for you. He has a love letter of hope written specifically for you—several, actually.

When you ask Him the hard questions, He will indeed give you the hard answers. Our dear and courageous sojourner of a friend named Paul hit the nail on the head many a time. One nugget of truth stood out to me today: "That I may know Him" (Philippians 3:10 NASB).

That we may *know* Him. That we may know the Creator of the universe and the Savior of our souls. Not know about Him. Not know of Him. But to *know* Him. A note from the NASB

Study Bible speaks to this verse: "Knowing Christ Jesus. Not only a knowledge of facts but a knowledge gained through experience that, in its surpassing greatness, transforms the entire person ... this knowledge is not merely factual."

He desires so deeply to know us. He knows that without Him in our lives, leading and sustaining us, we are doomed. Not just postmortem, but in the here and now. Without Him, our lives can never be lived abundantly or fully. He wants us to know Him and seek His heart because that is the best thing that could ever happen to us, so much so that He has done and will do whatever it takes to get us on our knees, gazing into His love-filled face while crying out to Him. He acts not out of selfishness but out of pure joy, pure passion, and pure faithfulness to His children.

If you keep reading in this chapter of Philippians, you see more of the bigger picture laid out by our King.

> That I may know Him and the power of His resurrection and the fellowship of His sufferings, being conformed to His death; in order that I may attain to the resurrection from the dead. (Philippians 3:10–11)

By knowing Him, we gain His power. We die the death of ourselves, the flesh that wars against the holy, the flesh that demands a trouble-free life void of any mountain or heartache, the flesh that only focuses on the temporary and is blind to the eternal. This flesh cannot handle the worrisome seasons because it is in no way rooted in the totality of Jesus Christ. This flesh only has eyes for one thing: itself, without the compassion or trace of a thought toward others. This flesh leads a life void of joy that overcomes. It's void of hope that presses on with the assurance of good to come. It's void of the only thing that will ever quench that insatiable thirst that plagues us all: Jesus.

By knowing Him, He gives us the understanding that He is our deepest need and most treasured prize. He is our true love and our home.

And, sister, if you are struggling with believing that and leaning on the Holy of Holies, it's okay. I've been there. If you cannot see past your circumstances and are so angry with this hand you've been dealt, there is hope, a Helper. I pray you hear Jesus instead of me right now.

Call on His name. Ask Him for a desire to want to know Him above all else. Ask Him to be worth more than this temporary life. Ask Him to open your spiritual ears and eyes to all of who He is. At the end of the day, when all is said and done, only He can make you whole. Only He can make you sing, "Hallelujah," when your heart is broken.

You know how I know this? Because He did exactly that for me many times. And He did it for Paul.

He let me see that all of this life, all the good and all the not-so-good, has beauty. No road is perfect. No journey is void of pain. But, oh, how I have a radiant hope in the Painter of the sunsets and the Forgiver of my heinous ways. He is above all and inhabits all, if you let Him.

He showed me to stop looking at what I don't have and start focusing on what I do have, the biggest and best being Him. Sister, He wants you—all of you, right now, in this crummy circumstance.

The wise man Paul also said, "Now I want you to know, brethren, that my circumstances have turned out for the greater progress of the gospel" (Philippians 1:12 NASB). Now, there is a man who had it rough. Yet he delighted in the fact that his sufferings gave him the opportunity to share the gospel. How is that possible? By the grace and mercy of Jesus. He transformed Paul's mind and redeemed his soul to sing "Hallelujah" when he was in jail, or shipwrecked, or beaten. Spend some time in Acts if you want to see some hardcore suffering.

Our circumstances are exactly that: circumstances. They're not identity, and they're not forever. They're not life. They're merely external happenings intended by a merciful God to draw you closer to His heart. In all the days we are given, let our hearts long more for the one who made them than for anything else that won't give us peace.

> All the commandments that I am commanding you today you shall be careful to do, that you may live and multiply, and go in and possess the land which the Lord swore to give to your forefathers. You shall remember all the way which the Lord your God has led you in the wilderness these forty years, that He might humble you, testing you, to know what was in your heart, whether you would keep His commandments or not. He humbled you and let you be hungry, and fed you with manna which you did not know, nor did your fathers know, that He might make you understand that man does not live by bread alone, but man lives by everything that proceeds out of the mouth of the Lord. (Deuteronomy 8:1–3 NASB)

We don't live by our circumstances alone. We don't thrive on sunny days, and we don't wilt on overcast seasons. We are not satisfied by what the world deems suitable to give us joy and contentment. Having Jesus means that every little thing about us, around us, and within us—all comes from Him. And in Him is the true life.

I want you, dear girl, to smile. Maybe not today, and maybe not this week, but soon. I want you to be able to genuinely smile and say, "I know Him … and I love Him." Even when your heart has just been broken. Even when you have to clean out the gutters by yourself. Even if you have to kill that demonic spider in your house. And even if everyone around you gives you pity looks and approves of your bitterness and wallowing. I pray that in those moments, you will confidently look that circumstance in the eye, take a deep breath, and proclaim to the heavenlies, "Hallelujah, Jesus is mine. Oh, how I know Him. And, oh, how He has good for me. Good in Him. By Him. From Him. For Him. Jesus is mine."

Maybe, just maybe, a fellow heartbroken sister will hear your song and see your smile that you let Jesus work so hard to give you. Maybe she will call upon this Jesus of ours and begin the journey to being made whole and knowing Him like we once began. Give us grace, Jesus.

# It's Time to Live and Live Abundantly

Dear Single Girl,

This life has so many seasons. Physically, we have winter, spring, summer, and fall. In sports we have offseason, preseason, playoffs, and finals. In the media and entertainment arena, we have fall seasons of shows, summer seasons of shows, and of course the numbered seasons. I mean, who doesn't love catching up on the current season of their favorite show? And when the devout fans are forced to wait until fall for the next season to air, oh, what agony. People impatiently await the outcome of the previous cliffhanger, missing their favorite characters and the plots that grab and hold their attention.

For the in between, what do most of us do? We find a different show to fill our time, or we fill our time with something else besides television. Maybe it's not by choice, but our neglected interests now hold our attention once again. That bookshelf gets dusted off, and we dive into the pages of that book that captivates the soul. Our tennis shoes get use once more as we pound the pavement or tarry on those woodsy trails. Our kitchen welcomes us as we spend more time creating a masterpiece rather than a rushed or thrown-together meal. Our crafty side appears, and our homes and friends are blessed with the creativity that buzzes inside us. Even our yards are a little more manicured and tidy because let's be real: what else do we have to do?

Maybe it's just me. Maybe I'm the only one who still follows shows as they air. Maybe I'm the only weird one who prioritizes an hour (or several) of my time to find out who falls in love or who dies this week on certain shows. Maybe I'm the only one who gets emotionally invested in the lives of fictional characters and weeps when they weep.

But in all seriousness, the life we have been given does have seasons as well. For you and me, my dear, sweet, dateless friend, ours currently has the quality of a lonely season. Now, I don't intend for lonely to be taken in a negative context. I simply say it for what it is: one person, doing life as a single girl. Sure, we still have our families, our friends, our community, and so many other people around us. But we don't have our built-in best friend. However, if you have been hearing me through all these letters, we have our Jesus. He's the only one to truly matter. He trumps all else.

Now, if I were talking to you face-to-face in this moment, the inflection of my voice is one of objectivity. I am not whining. I am not bitter in my tone. I am simply being real. This single season is what it is. I hope by now that what I am about to say will land right in your heart, where it needs to be.

*Let's enjoy it.*

Let's enjoy every minute of it. Let's ask Jesus to tune our hearts to songs of joy and delight. Let's ask Him to give us eyes that look at our lives through filters of grace, peace, and worship. Let's look at the loneliness that is a fact in our lives and say, "Oh, praise You, Father, for another day to walk with You and You alone," instead of remaining needy and desperate girls paralyzed by what we don't have. Let's stop dwelling on all the negatives and see the good laid before us.

Sister, I hate to break it to you, but every season of life from here on out has an element of waiting and the opportunity to be discontent. It may be shocking to know that once someone is off the market, the loneliness could still be there.

What are you going to do if your husband has to travel for a week, and you're left at home alone?

What will you say if one of you gets a new job nine hours from your mom, sister, or best friend?

What will you do when you realize your husband is a stinky man who doesn't want to hold your hand while you take a long, romantic walk at dusk, and he would rather watch the Thunder beat the Warriors?

Lord forbid if, on your anniversary, you make a huge dinner and dessert, shave your legs, wear a new and flattering dress, and prepare a handwritten letter to your beloved … and he gets called into work late. Then he doesn't get home until after you have gone to sleep.

How will you react if you don't get pregnant right away?

What will you do if one of your children has a health problem or simply won't sleep through the night?

What will you do when your husband is out of town, and the shower curtain rod falls again?

Now, I am not speaking any of this over you. I simply want you to realize that not being single will in no way make all of life's problems disappear.

Waiting is a hallmark of living. How we use that time is where life can be truly lived. All of us have mountains. All of us have what-ifs. All of us have wishes for a different story. But all of us have been planted right here by the one who waters our souls.

Life is beautiful in all seasons. We simply have to seek the beautiful life Jesus has for each one of us. He will give you the grace to love the lonely if you let Him. Jesus breeds contentment. Period.

I've had to do a lot of asking for grace-filtered eyes, believe me. But you know what? He's given me those eyes. He's given me opportunities to see the good part of the lonely. When I look at the empty side of my queen bed, I'm thankful I don't have to share my covers or have my sleep interrupted by snoring. When there is no one home with me late at night when I just need to talk through something, my Jesus is always ready to listen and be my wise Counselor. When I have to make a big decision, it is a relief to know that my Jesus is my Husband who will shed some light and has given me some wise people who invest in my big decisions.

When I need to stay late at work and be a listening ear for a worn-out mama or broken coworker, thankfully I am not making a husband wait on me. When I look around my home and notice the absence of masculinity on my walls, in my cabinets, and within the bare refrigerator, I usually take a deep breath and smile quietly at the flowers and the banners that have overtaken everything. This single-girl house is very much a girl house, from the pink and floral bedroom to the pantry that houses chick food. Honestly, I wouldn't have it any other way.

As silly and shallow as these perspectives may be, I truly mean all of them. I like my alone time. With this time, I have been able to connect with the Lord in ways I absolutely know would not have happened if I was a *we* and not a *me*.

> For your husband is your Maker, whose name is the Lord of hosts; and your Redeemer is the Holy One of Israel, who is called the God of all the earth. (Isaiah 54:5 NASB)

Sister, if anything, this lonely season is no longer considered lonely to me. This is my beautiful story Jesus has for me. Every day,

I choose to not be defined by my singleness. It is the reality I live, and it is 100 percent ordained by the Lord. Even with the spiders, the nasty trash can, the burned-out light bulbs, and the cursed shower curtain rods, I am in His will. Sure, I'm waiting. But I am also living. I could give you a rundown of what my days look like, but I don't want you to compare and feel as though you should lead a life like mine. This is my story. What is your story, sweet girl?

Whether that means learning how to sew, running a marathon, joining a ladies' Bible study, going on a mission trip, joining a Zumba class, investing your time into others, writing a book, going to school, or even learning to cook—whatever it looks like to you, it is time to start joyously living. Stop feeling sorry for yourself.

Look around you. Those trees outside really are a work of the Lord's artistic ability and design. That sunset? Wow, radiant. That fact that your heart (hopefully) is searching and seeking more of Jesus? Hallelujah. By seeking Him, He will open your eyes to your story. He will help you see the grace in the lonely. He will speak to the very depths of your heart that have felt so empty. He will fulfill you and keep you and take care of you. Now, it's time to live and enjoy this moment.

Life is hard. But it is equally beautiful if we surrender our hopes and ideas of what a good and happy life should look like. Come sit at His feet and let go of your demands. Relinquish your ultimatums and crucify the bitterness because your life is different. Praise God your life is different. He wants you to be unique because He has mighty plans for you. Jesus is the Captain. He knows that best route and holds the map for your greatest adventure. Let your compass point to Him and enjoy this voyage. It is the only one you have; don't wish it away.

> I will lead the blind by a way they do not know, in paths
> they do not know I will guide them. I will make darkness

into light before them and rugged places into plains. These are the things I will do, and I will not leave them undone. (Isaiah 42:16 NASB)

Until it is time for that next season of our show to come back on air, I pray we all see the beauty in the time given to us. It's time our Captain set aside to let us get to know Him and an abundant life away from what the world deems worthy.

You know, I'm learning that there is so much freedom enjoying my time now rather than pining for that picture-perfect man with muscles for days. When my days are not dictated by expectations, the waiting disappears, and abundance and peace start to rise. Social stereotypes fall. Bitterness and despair crumble. Pure joy springs forth.

Let's enjoy this journey. Every second. I promise you won't be disappointed.

And you will know that I am the Lord; those who hopefully wait for Me will not be put to shame. (Isaiah 49:23c NASB)

*Alyssa Phillips*

# *Lacking Nothing*

Dear Single Girl,

I hope you have had a good day today. Actually, I hope all of your days are good, but I know that every day cannot always be a good day. Some days are harder than others, so I pray that as this letter finds you today, you are having a good day, or it will make a lovely shift into a beautiful day.

As I was sitting on my back porch on this hot June evening, the Lord reminded me of a little but mighty nugget of truth, and I think He would like you to be reminded as well. You have to share those truth nuggets with your sisters.

As the sun shone upon me and the sweet songbirds made their melodies, the Lord whispered into my soul, "You aren't lacking anything."

It was as if He came and sat next to me, put His hand over mine, and peacefully smiled while offering that truthful sentiment.

I repeated it to myself. *I'm not lacking anything.*

I then tried to counter it with my list of *have-nots* and *losses*. With each bullet point, He met me tit for tat.

I've lost my mom, Lord.
*She's with Me. You're en route to her and Me. I am with you always.*

Behold, I am with you and will keep you wherever you go, and will bring you back to this land; for I will not leave you until I have done what I have promised you. (Genesis 28:15 NASB)

I've ended the relationship with a man I
could have potentially married.
*I ended that for your benefit and for Mine. He is not
yours. I am your Companion and Comfort.*

For your husband is your Maker, whose name is the Lord of hosts; and your Redeemer is the Holy One of Israel, who is called God of all the earth. (Isaiah 54:5 NASB)

I have no children of my own.
*Your time is coming. I have given you abundant life, even
in this season of waiting and learning contentment.*

Behold, God is my salvation, I will trust and not be afraid; for the Lord God is my strength and my song, and He has become my salvation. Therefore you will joyously draw water from the springs of salvation. (Isaiah 12:2–3 NASB)

I have no five-year plan.
*I have a plan already written for you, My child.
I am your plan, your foundation.*

But just as it is written, "Things which eye has not seen and ear has not heard, and which have not entered the heart of man, all that God has prepared for those who love Him." (1 Corinthians 2:9 NASB)

This was my list, just to name a few. With each loss, the Lord answered quickly with a gain in Him.

How easy it is to compile our lists of *lacks*. Sure, when you compare your life to someone else, you will come up short in different areas. I am not going to recite the cliché "The grass is always greener on the other side" because every yard is different—different season, different storm, different restoration, different growing season.

Sister, Jesus has you right here, right now, for something beautiful. In this yard of yours, you lack nothing. If Jesus has found you and rescued you from sin and darkness, you lack nothing. You have every tool, seed, soil type, and water supply to blossom right where your feet are planted. If you don't think you do, or if you don't know how to grow in your circumstances, then get on those strong knees of yours and ask Him.

> For God, who said, 'Light shall shine out of darkness,' is the One who has shone in our hearts to give the Light of the knowledge of the glory of God in the face of Christ. (2 Corinthians 4:6 NASB)

Ask Him how. Ask Him how to bloom in the midst of your disparities. Ask Him to bring someone to do life with you and counsel you. Ask Him for an example of a woman who does life soundly with Jesus. Ask Him to fix it. Whatever it is that is keeping you from showing off those beautiful blossoms of grace and confidence that the Lord has intended for you to display, ask Him to illuminate the root of darkness. Ask Him to remove it and to fill that void with His Word, His power, His Spirit, His love.

Sister, let's ask Him to be the Boss of our gardens, and let's do whatever it takes to cultivate healthy soil free of deception, strongholds, distractions, and fears. Let's ask Him to kill off the weeds so our hearts can truly see the good in the midst of our lists of losses. We need not ask Him to change our circumstances; those will shift soon enough. We need to ask Him to change ourselves.

> But we have this treasure in earthen vessels, so that the surpassing greatness of the power will be of God and not from ourselves; we are afflicted in every way, but not crushed; perplexed but not despairing; persecuted, but not forsaken; struck down, but not destroyed; always carrying about in the body the dying of Jesus, so that the life of Jesus also may be manifested in our body. For we who live are constantly being delivered over to death for Jesus' sake, so that the life of Jesus also may be manifested in our mortal flesh. So death works in us, but life in you. (2 Corinthians 4:7-12 NASB)

If our list of loss is great, the power and strength of Jesus will be tenfold—and then some.

Only He can renew our minds. Only He can deliver us from comparison. Only He can give us contentment in all seasons. Only He can let us confidently say, "I truly lack nothing."

Only He can make us new. Not better—new. He makes us new by pruning the dead. He doesn't make the dead part of our gardens better. He brings in a whole new crop and seed.

My prayer for you, dear friend whom I've never met, is this:

> And the Lord will continually guide you, and satisfy your desire in scorched places, and give strength to your bones; and you will be like a watered garden, and like a spring of water whose waters do not fail. (Isaiah 58:11 NASB)

He is our only hope. He is our only rescue. He is the only way to survive your season of singleness and blossom into a secure, content, unafraid and graceful lady. Ready to face whatever each day will bring. All the while knowing that, like Paul, we too can want for nothing.

> Not that I speak from want, for I have learned to be content in whatever circumstances I am. (Philippians 4:11 NASB)

> And my God will supply all your needs according to His riches in glory in Christ Jesus. (Philippians 4:19 NASB)

# Let's Be Encouraged

Dear Single Girl,

Just a short, sweet letter for you today that hinges on a single verse from Paul to the Church in Rome.

> That is, that I may be encouraged together with you while among you, each of us by the others faith, both yours and mine. (Romans 1:12 NASB)

Oh, how I wish I could be sitting across from you so I could see your beautiful face. I dearly wish I could be holding a cup of fresh black coffee and sharing brunch with you. I don't know you. I don't know what you look like. I don't know what makes you laugh or what stings your expressive eyes with tears. I may never meet you. But just know, sweet friend, that I love you and am praying the sweetness of Jesus and His fully encompassing peace will be so real and dear to you. I want so badly to look you in the eye and be the mouthpiece of Jesus. I want to hear your story, your faith, and your life, and I equally want to be blessed by a kindred spirit. It goes both ways, you know—the whole imparting wisdom and receiving wisdom. It's a constant ebb and flow of giving and accepting. It is even sweeter when it is the Lord initiating it all.

I love Paul's life, even the messiness of it, the taboo and the distasteful. But what I really love is how desperately he loves Jesus and intentionally loves His church. It's a love that bears, that invests, that listens, that does not bat an eye at the struggles and shame attached to this life on this side of heaven. He purely and simply loves people while seeing Jesus work in people. It's so simple yet so profound. His life was totally transformed into one of always being about the Lord's business. He led such a unique life that many won't have the opportunity to mimic it, and that's okay. But I don't think the unusualness of his life should be overlooked.

I believe he was doing his best at following in the footsteps of his Savior. And in that, there is mighty beauty and grace. Even in the unconventional and otherworldly, I think it is in our best interest to learn several lessons from Paul's life. But this letter is not about his entire life. It is about this simple verse that shows his character and reveals a nugget of grace for you and for me.

He desires fellowship and physical closeness with this body of believers. He craves to be encouraged by their faith. It's as simple as that.

Something special happens when soul sisters and soul brothers get together. If the Spirit of the Lord is invited in, oh, what goodness and life can come forth from these gatherings. When life is spoken, when Jesus is made much of, when testimonies of His faithfulness grace our lips, when burdens are admitted and shared, when raw and pleading prayers are prayed—this is where redemption can exist. These moments create the freedom for sanctification and the space for abounding grace.

Talking about the Lord brings life.

Bragging on the good He's done brings life.

Being honest about your heart brings life.

Jesus uses our own stories to tell of His story. We must never forget His story in us and His desire to use us as a picture of His faithfulness.

Even when your heart is broken, listen to those who have been brought forth from the ashes. Better yet, choose to see beyond your despairing brokenness and tell of His unfailing love for you. Whether it's from a scripture, from something in your past, or from something in someone else's life, remember what He has done so you can trust in what He is going to do.

Today, I had the honor of getting to sit across the breakfast table from a precious soul who has been captivated by Jesus. She and I were able to tell of the goodness of the Lord in our lives despite the imperfections and past griefs.

Without having known each other's life stories, the Lord so sweetly knew each of us needed a little Romans 1:12. We needed to be encouraged and listen to a fellow single girl. We did not need to dwell on the singleness but rather dwell on His purposes for and through us right now, in this season. We needed to be reminded that the Lord has other precious souls we haven't met yet who will become part of our stories. We had to find some Jesus in the midst of darkness.

My prayer for you is that in the near future, the Lord will gift you with some encouragement. However that will look is up to the Lord, but I think Paul was on to something when he expressed his desire to be in close contact with his beloved believers. I bet he even wanted to be in touch with those he didn't know well and the ones who had yet to receive Christ. I pray that you will be pleasantly surprised with some refreshing encouragement. I pray that you're reminded there is so much more to life than your relationship status. God cares more for you than a future spouse ever will, and sometimes you need to sit and enjoy a conversation that sings of the Lord's goodness.

# Tear Down
# Our Idols

Dear Single Girl,

I want to share with you something the Lord has shared with me. It's one of those lessons that is needed but not always talked about. I will begin this letter to you with a portion of my prayer journal entry from several months ago.

> August 27, 2018
>
> You're showing me that I have, in ways, idolized dating and marriage. It has been a goal of mine, a huge desire. And Lord, has it become an idol? My current life will not stop when I get married. My circles won't change, and my ministry cannot cease. It will be a gift, an addition to my story, but not the end. Not the final chapter, but another door to walk through. More change. More challenges. But my dependence on You, my being filled in You, my walk with You cannot be severed when a man arrives. Such a learning curve.

Lord, tear down the high places of idolship of a relationship, an engagement, and a marriage. What culture sells, what the movies sell, is false security. Worshipping the marriage isn't okay. A man becoming my only person and isolating me from others—not okay. Jesus, thank You for rescuing me from that. Let me desire a friendship and a healthy friend-infused, community-centered relationship, a group-oriented and family-tilted dating relationship. Show him and I how to do it right. Let the alone time be kept somewhat minimal for purity's sake.

Let Your intention for a relationship and marriage be my heart's desire. Bring me a man whom I can trust to spiritually protect and go to battle for me. You know what I need. Work on him like You're working on me. Prune the unholy. Heal the brokenness. Give us both eyes to see You. Let our hearts stay separate until marriage. How quickly I let my guard down sometimes. Jesus, be big within and around me. I need Your grace.

The Lord reminded me on this day that the world around me has been selling marriage in a way that He never intended. The world is selling ideals and dreams that take away from who God is and who He is for us.

Not once in Scripture does He promise us girls that a knight in shining armor will rescue us. He promises us that *He* will rescue us. Not once in Scripture does He promise us a man's love that will heal, protect, and satisfy our hearts. He promises us that *He* will heal, protect, and satisfy our deepest needs. Not once in Scripture does He promise a happy ending due to falling in love with that handsome guy. He promises us that *He* is our happy ending, even in the midst of dark days and tribulations.

Our hearts were created to be pursued, protected, and cherished. Jesus is the one who does this perfectly. No man will ever rise to the standard that the Lord has set. That is exactly the way He intended life to be lived. He intentionally made us imperfect so His perfection and holiness would be on display. Our love stories were never intended to be written where the man himself is the final answer to our prayers. The Lord's goodness, provision, and life should be the utmost answer.

Now, don't hear what I am not saying. I fully believe that the Lord does hear and answer prayers by bringing godly men to women's lives, and vice versa. What a gift these relationships and marriages are. But when the focus remains on the human qualities and fleshly aspects, that is where man becomes the idol. He steals God's glory. What a scary thing. It may not be blatantly obvious, but those idols are created without us even knowing it.

The idol of believing that once you are married, life will finally be good. *Life is good now with Jesus at the center.*

The idol of needing a man to feel loved and cherished. *Jesus loves you better and stronger than any man ever could.*

The idol of having a perfect love story to share with your grandkids one day. *The story of the gospel will be the most beautiful and eternal story worth sharing.*

The idol of needing to be married to feel accepted in this culture. *Because of the cross, Jesus accepts you, single or married, and will never reject you like the world around you will.*

The idol of believing that your life will be worth something once you are married. *Jesus has given you today a purpose to be a light and share this light, even without a wedding band on your finger.*

The list of idols could continue forever, but I hope you get what I am saying. There are so many thoughts we all have but don't necessarily talk about. There are deep beliefs that our hearts long for. There are seasons we wish would arrive sooner rather than later. There is nothing wrong with having a desire to be married, but there is something wrong when that is our main desire of life. If it overshadows knowing Jesus and walking with Him right where He has us, then it is time to start taking inventory of some idols in our hearts.

In the Old Testament, the people of God were so often drawn to the idols of the cultures around them. There were literal idols and literal temples dedicated to gods other than their God Almighty. One of many examples of a king rebelling against the sovereignty of God is that of Manasseh.

> Manasseh was twelve years old when he became king, and he reigned fifty-five years in Jerusalem. He did evil in the sight of the Lord according to the abominations of the nations whom the Lord dispossessed before the sons of Israel. For he rebuilt the high places which Hezekiah his father had broken down; he also erected altars for the Baals and made Asherim, and worshipped all the host of heaven and served them. He built altars in the house of the Lord of which the Lord said, "My name shall be in Jerusalem forever." For he built altars for all the host of heaven in the two courts of the house of the Lord. (2 Chronicles 33:1–6 NASB)

A biblical scholar I am not, but I am one to pay attention to those who have done evil in the sight of the Lord, with all of the implications and consequences involved. This guy Manasseh placed so many things at the same level as God Almighty. He called his nation, the people of God, to abandon their identity as pure God worshippers and to adopt extra deities and customs outside of the Holy One. He led Judah down a scary path of destruction, outside of the will of God. What a dark time for those people. My heart is heavy for the ones who, by sheer grace, remained faithful and withstood the culture shift within their communities. The king of their land was blatantly rebelling against what was right, and so were the people next to them. They saw the dark turns and lifeless deities. They saw the downfall of sin among them. They saw the tolerance of sin that coexisted with worship and the law. They saw it all. Sounds eerily familiar to our current culture, doesn't it?

Now, this letter is not about this day and age with its counterscriptural ways of grace abusing, sin exalting, and tolerance-promoting sermons within the Church. No, this letter is about idols within our own hearts that destroy and bring death. These idols replace the fullness of the holy God. They that creep into our homes and catch us unaware.

Friend, take a moment and think about your own heart. It may not be one that worships other gods. It may not be one that shoves its fist at Jesus and says, "You're not enough. Let's add the Baals back into the mix." It may not be one that practices evil and breeds rebellion. But what about your desires? What about your goals? What about your security? If the answer to any of those is something other than Jesus, His provision, His business, and His cross, then it is time to let Him restore what is dark, broken, and lost.

Idol worship has many faces and is so much more than having a shrine with weird candles and evil statues. Idol worship begins deep within us as soon as we believe that something other than the totality of God can bring us fulfilling joy and life. It starts small and snowballs into something heartbreaking. You can't compartmentalize who God is. You cannot say, "He is my provision and my source of financial stability," but in the same breath whisper, "But He clearly is late in bringing me a man I can share life with, so I am going to take care of this one myself." You cannot trust Him for His atoning blood without trusting Him for your future life. You cannot trust Him for food on your table and not trust Him for the ability to prepare a man for you. You cannot trust Him for joy in the hard times and then question His purpose for your life. He is either all good, all providing, and all faithful, or He is none of those things. He isn't a God who provides half of what we need. He provides it all. And don't forget that what we really need usually differs from what we want.

> If you then, being evil, know how to give good gifts to your children, how much more will your heavenly Father give the Holy Spirit to those who ask Him? (Luke 11:13 NASB)

What He offers us is enough, period. The second you or I begin to question this and assume otherwise, the spiral of idol worship will ensue.

You're not dating anyone? Good. Trust in His plan for this season. Don't get on those online dating websites and start talking to strangers. You are meant to be single right now.

You're not married? Good. Let Him prepare you for the challenging seasons to come. Don't pine away for that perfect marriage, perfect family, and perfect house. Those don't exist.

You're alone on Friday and Saturday night? Good. Thank Him that He is protecting you from spiraling into a path of sin and destruction and away from His heart.

In order to remove the idols from within our hearts, we first must recognize what the idols actually are. Indeed, they are idols: Coveting what those around you have. Making your life goal to be a wife and a mother. Not patiently waiting on the Lord to do His job at providing. All of this reeks of discontentment, mistrust, self-ability, and self-glory. If Jesus and His ways are not more important to you than one day having the perfect white dress, that white dress may be an idol to you. If seeing the lost found and the sinner freed is not as high on your priority list as wanting perfect family pictures, that dream may be an idol. If hearing of the goodness of the Lord is not as soul-satisfying as holding hands with a man, that man may be your idol.

We must be cautious to keep the gifts of the Lord in their rightful place below Him, as gifts. He is our treasure. He is our satisfaction. He is our hope. At least, that is what He intends us to sing and believe. I pray that your eyes are open to the corners of your heart and that you surrender what has taken its place as god in your own life. It may be subtle and small, but a little bit of darkness can go a long way.

After Manasseh did his thing and brought havoc on Judah, a king several years after him began to seek the Lord and obeyed His desire for His kingdom.

> Josiah was eight years old when he became king, and he reigned thirty-one years in Jerusalem. He did right in the sight of the Lord, and walked in the ways of his father David and did not turn aside to the right or to the left. For in the eighth year of his reign while he was still a youth, he began to seek the God of his father David; and in the twelfth year he began to purge Judah and Jerusalem of the high places, the Asherim, the carved images and the molten images. They tore down the altars of the Baals in his presence, and the incense altars that were high above them he chopped down; also the Asherim, the carved images and the molten images he broke in pieces and ground to powder and scattered it on the graves of those who had sacrificed to them. (2 Chronicles 34:1–4 NASB)

Josiah was serious about making things right. He left no room for darkness. He left no stone unturned and completely restored the evil to goodness. He obeyed God and took Him seriously when He so often commanded His people to love Him and choose Him over the temptations around them.

I call heaven and earth to witness against you today, that I have set before you life and death, the blessing and the curse. So choose life in order that you may live, you and your descendants, by loving the Lord your God, by obeying His voice, and by holding fast to Him; for this is your life and the length of your days, that you may live in the land which the Lord swore to your fathers, to Abraham, Isaac, and Jacob, to give them. (Deuteronomy 30:19–20 NASB)

Sister, it does not get more straightforward than that. We have a choice. Choose life, or choose death. Choose God, or choose false security and real darkness. Choose to obey, or choose to suffer. I cannot make this choice for you. I can simply pray that you will see the severity of holding on to idols, as small as they may be, and what they will indeed do to your life. From clinging to idols, mistrust is born. From ignoring idols, sin strongholds are born. From walking in the path of your idol, walking out of God's will is born.

If anyone needs to read this letter, it is me. Like I said at the beginning, the Lord is showing me this. As crazy as it may seem and as countercultural as it appears, He is right. Even the smallest of idols will take us down. Even the dreams and desires that are from Him can be magnified above Him if we let them. I pray we are not like Manasseh or his followers. I pray we deeply evaluate our hearts and let God uproot the idols that take precedence over loving Him and being loved by Him. I pray we do not ignore the warnings He gives and choose life from Him over deception from the world. I pray He gives us the desire to stay so closely in His will that one wrong step or one misplaced desire brings us to our knees before His throne. He will restore our high places as His dwelling place forever. O Jesus, rescue us from the idols and dreams that have taken away your glory and goodness.

# *Jesus,*
# *Take the Wheel*

Dear Precious Friend,

By now we have spent some time together. You've continued to read these letters that have been written for you. I pray you have heard Jesus more than me. I pray your single girl heart is slowly beginning to shake off the title of *single girl* and hold up the banner of *beautiful, loved, cherished, and taken care of.* My biggest prayer for you, and for all the other girls who are married, dating, engaged, and more, is a prayer that pleas with Jesus to open up your eyes and ears to Him. Boldly open up your entire heart, from the deepest corners of shame to the space you've thought to reserve only for that man, so your beautifully precious heart is open wide for your Jesus. He will not disappoint.

Now, we have shared many hours and pages discussing the overwhelming aspects of this independent life. I want to encourage you in a new way today, not in any way dismissing what overwhelms you. When the numbers in that checking account are not adding up, when your car needs new tires and an oil change, when that cursed shower curtain rod keeps falling down and all the profanities come forth from you with lightning speed, you should kneel by a pew while *every knee is bowed and every eye is closed.* Yeah, that is still real life. I'm in that old church house next to you once again, repenting and silently cursing the inventor of those shower curtain rods.

O Jesus, take the wheel.

Let's be real. That phrase spews out of my mouth more that I care to admit. I would like to think I am so theologically deep and scripturally competent that I am merely paraphrasing 1 Peter 5:7, "Casting all your anxiety on Him, because He cares for you."

Clearly the heart intent is the same. Oh, how anxiety is alive and well. And, oh, how He cares for me. I would also like to think that my exasperated moments that test the purity of my speech and thoughts slightly amuse Him. When I am staring at my car after a tire blew out—and the wheel may or may not have blown off too. When I'm staring so intently trying to figure out how to fix this with my newly painted nails and cute tote bag full of pens, lip gloss, gum, and lotion, not tools. I hope He has a giggle or two. Or when that spider wants to make nice and have a slumber party. How the heavens are roaring from that one.

As much as I get overwhelmed and in a tizzy, usually several times in one day, Jesus smiles and calmly tells me, "I've got you. I will indeed take the wheel from you, Alyssa. Because, My precious hot mess, I've had the wheel the entire time. I would not dream of letting you down."

Oh, how sweet my Jesus is. And you know what that is, my friend? That is a transformed heart and mind right there. He shifts the focus from the disparity, the negative, and incapability and turns my head to Him. There's nothing sweeter than locking eyes with the Beloved. He makes all things right. He makes all things good. He lets me see the beauty in each day, regardless of the smoke and dust billowing from the disaster in my life. And He can do the same for you.

Each year for the last few years, I have had a theme for that year, a theme of my life, a theme given to me by Jesus. I've had a mantra of sorts that defines that year and depicts exactly what my soul needed along the way. In 2016, my theme was "Thinking like Jesus." Underwhelming, right? I know it is far less exciting than "Best Year Yet" or "A Year of New Adventure and Love."

Thinking like Jesus. Letting Him put a filter in my mind to compare thoughts with His truth. Dismissing any idea that does not measure up and asking it to never come back. Romans 12:2 articulates it well.

> And do not be conformed to this world, but be transformed by the renewing of your mind, so that you may prove what the will of God is, that which is good and acceptable and perfect.

A new mind. At salvation, when Jesus plucks us out of the holy wrath and wipes us clean with His blood, He makes us new and lets our spirits come to life. It's a deep awakening from within by this passionate Father. Along with that comes a new mind. It is like Christmas morning for your soul. But with any new gift, declutter and cleaning out the old must come. Yes, we have new minds, but there are lingering thought processes, habits, lies, and cobwebs all up in that business. That's why the verb context says *renewing*. To think like Jesus and to have the mind of Christ—this is a process.

I don't mean a twelve-step process. Multiply that by eighty-five, and that is more realistic. Having the mind of Christ takes time and grit. It takes sitting down alone with the Lord and asking Him to expose the fleshly remnants in that noggin of yours. It takes shining His holy light on the thinking that is not from

Him, isn't for Him, and isn't okay with Him. It takes repeating Scripture countless times and preaching that to yourself until it becomes a pillar of your soul. It takes rebuking lies and calling out darkness with the authority of the Cross.

Grit, I'm telling you: grit.

It is no easy feat, but it is an essential hurdle we must face and overcome. And believe me, it isn't "Poof! I finally made it. My mind is transformed." Wrong.

Until the day we meet Jesus face-to-face, our minds will continually need to be transformed. We walk and breathe in a broken and desperately fallen world. We are always subject to attack. But don't misunderstand me here. None of us will ever arrive and be done, but we can and will have victory in our minds. Jesus will change your thinking if you let Him. If you choose to dwell in the reality of His truth and promises, you will think like Him. When the temptation comes to fall back into the dark hole of depraved thoughts, you proclaim with confidence who Jesus is, that you are a new and beautiful creation, and that you won't have anything to do with worldly thinking. That was then, and this is now.

> Therefore if anyone is in Christ, he is a new creature; the old things passed away; behold, new things have come. (2 Corinthians 5:17 NASB)

Let me be practical. I tend to overanalyze and rethink something until I've thought of about 866 possibilities and alternatives. Sometimes—most of the time—that superpower is used for harm instead of good. I have a hard time just letting it go. Can I get an amen?

But. I know, I know. *But.* This is not how believers should exercise their minds. Jesus didn't save us from darkness so we would continue to second-guess, to mistrust, to be easily swayed, or to believe false truths about ourselves, our lives, or our God.

For though we walk in the flesh, we do not war according to the flesh, for the weapons of our warfare are not of the flesh, but divinely powerful for the destruction of fortresses. We are destroying speculations and every lofty thing raised up against the knowledge of God, and we are taking every thought captive to the obedience of Christ. (2 Corinthians 10:3–5 NASB)

Finally, brethren, whatever is true, whatever is honorable, whatever is right, whatever is pure, whatever is lovely, whatever is of good repute, if there is any excellence and if anything worthy of praise, dwell on these things. The things you have learned and received and heard and seen in me, practice these things, and the God of peace will be with you. (Philippians 4:8–9 NASB)

We are to inspect the thoughts that come from within us as well as from our surroundings. We must ask Jesus to illuminate the truth within them or the darkness lacing the edges. If only it were as easy as a game of True or False. I hear you asking, "How do I do this? How can I overcome my habitual thoughts?" By asking.

But if any of you lacks wisdom, let him ask of God, who gives to all generously and without reproach, and it will be given to him. But he must ask in faith without any doubting, for the one who doubts is like the surf of the sea, driven and tossed by the wind. For that man ought not to expect that he will receive anything from the Lord, being a double-minded man, unstable in all his ways. (James 1:5–8 NASB)

Our Jesus is ever so faithful to answer His children. Ask Him to show you the strongholds, the lies, the self-pity, the hopelessness, and the wayward thoughts that don't have a place on the solid rock of God. These thoughts have plagued you long enough and are in need of sanctification and redemption. They keep you from Jesus. These thoughts speak to your old self, your old ways, or the ways of your family that in no way define you. They that are rooted in sin, are a falsely misguided identity, and question the truth of the Cross.

Practically speaking, it is as simple as getting alone with the Lord—and maybe a trusted friend, mentor, or counselor—and having a dialogue with Him. It's asking for clarity, asking for discernment, and asking for specific truths to claim victory over your weaknesses. It's pulling out your Word and confessing the thoughts that don't agree with what God says about you, about Him, or about the true Champion of this world. Our minds must act as safe havens for the presence of the glory of God, and they cannot serve that purpose when the lifeblood of Christ hasn't washed it clean.

Sister, if we neglect to let the Lord refine us, cleanse our minds, and make us new each day, we will walk down the path of verse 8: "being a double-minded man, unstable in all his ways."

How we think, how we believe, how we process—this overflows into our lives. The choice is ours: stability or instability. The latter is easy, letting the enemy use you as a punching bag while filling your dear heart with shame, unbelief, doubts, and falsities. But the former is where the grit comes in. That is where Jesus is, ready to be that grit for you. He's taking up camp within you, lighting a fire, preparing the table, and giving you rest from the hike.

Now, if you're at all like me—and I suspect you are because you haven't given up on this letter collection—you tend to get lost in the midst of your thinking, unable to determine north from south. Here is the verse that Jesus whispers loudly to me time and time again for so many different seasons which is the lifeblood to my critically ill faith, the defibrillator for my near lifeless mind, and my soothing revival in the face of mortality.

Be still, and know that I am God. (Psalm 46:10 NIV)

Be still. The NASB, my preferred translation because the words are a little meatier, says *cease striving*. Say that a few times. That takes the weight off of you. The burden is no longer yours because you know that He is God. There is so much totality and ability in that eight-word phrase. Let it be rain to your parched soul.

He can give you the ability to think righteous and honorable thoughts in the face of overwhelming life craziness. He can give you a sound mind in the place of fear, gloom, and unbelief. He can give you laughter in the place of tears, hope in the place of believing you will be forever alone, joy in the day-to-day routine that forces you to say, "Jesus, take the wheel," all too often.

Living a life of praise given to you by Jesus. Singing anthems of peace, glory, rest, and strength when no one else wants to sing your song. Letting that *Hallelujah* rise up from the depths of your soul instead of hanging your head. Although there will always be a reason to grumble and complain, there will always be a reason to sing, "Hallelujah," and join in with the heavenlies above and the creation here below, and genuinely sing.

Hallelujah! For the Lord our God, the Almighty, reigns. (Revelation 19:6b NASB)

Oh, dear sister, how I want this for you. How I pray you gain a quiet mind, you don't let your disparities define you, and you fall so deeply in love with Jesus that nothing seems to matter except knowing Him well.

# Sweet Goodbyes

As I sit here staring out my window on this chilly November day, I take in a deep breath. The list of letters to you, my friend, has been completed. This journey we have been on together has come to a sweet end. I began scribbling my hopes and prayers for you over two years ago in these little floral journals, and here we are, using a real computer with a real keyboard.

I had no idea where the Lord would take these letters. I still don't. All I know is that the words He has given me needed to be written. Maybe they're just for me. Maybe they're just for you and no one else. But maybe they're for something different than I could have ever imagined. Regardless of where these letters end up or who reads them, I pray that Jesus will be at the center of each and every one. I pray He uses my ramblings and His Word to illuminate your need for Him. I pray that you deeply know how loved you are and that everything will be okay.

He gives us the seasons in our lives for reasons that we may never know. But just as the winter days are long and the crisp air bites at our noses, spring is always coming. The flowers will bloom once again. Hope is always there. His faithfulness will always show up. And even in the frigid winter days, there is such beauty in the warmth of a cozy home, in the picture-perfect snow that covers the land, and in the moments that force us to stay inside and rest. Whatever season you are in now, I pray that the beauty of it is apparent. Maybe it's different than you dreamed it would be, but nonetheless it is beautiful.

So, my precious friend, take heart. Jesus is near. He is willing and ready to bring you hope. He is writing your story for His good and glory. All the while, He's considering what your heart needs and desires. He's transforming you along the way, preparing you for His business, and restoring the wrong to right. Don't ever forget you are so loved.

—AP